SNAPSHOT:

Ship's Dentists

SNAPSHOT:
Ship's Dentists

WILLIAM M. TRENTLY

iUniverse, Inc.
Bloomington

SNAPSHOT: SHIP'S DENTISTS

iUniverse books may be ordered through booksellers or by contacting:

iUniverse
1663 Liberty Drive
Bloomington, IN 47403
www.iuniverse.com
1-800-Authors (1-800-288-4677)

Because of the dynamic nature of the Internet, any web addresses or links contained in this book may have changed since publication and may no longer be valid.

ISBN: 978-1-4620-3726-1 (pbk)
ISBN: 978-1-4620-3775-9 (ebk)

Printed in the United States of America

iUniverse rev. date: 07/21/2011

CONTENTS

In memory of William J. Trently (1932-2010),

my father and dear friend

INTRODUCTION

A snapshot is a brief impression or view of something at a particular moment. It is a casual photo made typically by an amateur with a small handheld camera. In this book I have taken a photograph to give a short, limited imprint of what I experienced from 1987 to 1990 while serving as a dental officer in the United States Navy. During those years, I was fortunate to have been exposed to a wide variety of duty stations and situations. Of course, another person would capture a different picture because each individual encounters his or her own unique adventure, but through mine you may extrapolate to imagine how other photos in an album might appear. In my particular snapshot, you will be introduced to a nautical and military culture having its own language, rich traditions, and guiding mission: to conduct combat operations in support of the national interest (Part One). You will get a sense of what it was like to work in a large dental clinic, as well as in a small one (Part Two). You will go to sea aboard an aircraft carrier (Part Three) and travel to exotic foreign shores (Part Four). You will hear a brief history of the Navy Dental Corps, spend a few months in a shipyard, and board a Soviet warship during the Cold War (Part Five). You will find camaraderie and patriotism, and a love of and fascination with the sea.

I describe the experience as an "adventure" because every day working in the Navy was an exciting or remarkable experience and you just never knew who or what would cross your path. *It's not just a job. It's an adventure*: that Navy slogan was absolutely accurate, in my opinion. There was no better way to describe it. There might be unannounced drills agitating the calm, or you could be suddenly assigned to a special project. There were always people coming and going, passing through your work spaces. You never knew what would be the joke or comical twist of the day. And sometimes when you awakened you were in port, other times you were at sea. It was truly a variety-filled adventure.

Occasionally, because of the dangerous nature of the Navy's mission, there could be destructive incidents that altered schedules in major ways. I recall one particular day in the Dental Department aboard the USS John F. Kennedy. Each of the seven dental chairs was occupied by a patient and everyone was going about his usual duties. "Sprig, I need one of those elephant-stomper condensers right now!" someone yelled out as the whirr of high-speed handpieces droned from two other rooms. "I'll need bitewings on Petty Officer Smith so we can get his annual exam out of the way," another voice directed. One sailor from the flight deck crew staggered down the ladder with a slightly swollen face and toothache. He checked in by signing the log. Chief Gonzalez reassured him he would be well taken care of, then inquired, "What's going on today up above?" The sailor, holding his hand to his aching jaw, answered, "Oh, just routine flight ops."

Several decks above, an S-3B Viking was guided across the flight deck into its launch position. That day, the sun was shining without obstruction from any clouds over the calm blue ocean. The crewmembers sat in position, awaiting launch.

Of the various kinds of aircraft that operated from United States carriers, the Viking had the job of searching for and destroying enemy submarines. It was computerized and able to collect, process, interpret and store antisubmarine warfare data. Its crew of four could remain airborne for greater than seven hours in any kind of weather. This aircraft carried a diverse assortment of ordnance: torpedoes, mines, depth charges, rockets, and missiles. It carried sonobuoy loads and had the capability to analyze and display underwater sounds and other data on TV displays. Its avionics system represented the most extensive, multi-mode, sophisticated application of electronic sensor and software technology in any tactical aircraft.

The jet aircraft was launched by the catapult. As it left the flight deck, it climbed gradually into the air ahead of the carrier just as it was supposed to do, but then began a descent that indicated something was deadly wrong. Within seconds the Viking crashed into the water. Immediately, emergency rescue procedures were begun. The Medical Department was informed of the mishap. Because Dental was closely allied to Medical, its personnel reported to the medical spaces just up the ladder and prepared to assist.

Soon the rescue team recovered a pilot. I stood at the entrance to Main Medical and saw the badly contorted body of one of the victims carried in on a stretcher. Unfortunately, he was dead from his injuries. A few minutes later, another Viking crew member was rushed in. Several dental technicians obtained supplies and helped keep traffic moving unhindered. The team of doctors and corpsmen efficiently and swiftly began to stabilize the airman. Although severely injured, he was to survive. Outside the confines of the vessel, the rescue squad struggled for a long time but, sadly, could not recover the third and fourth men, who were dragged down with the heavy metal aircraft to the ocean's depths. I remember thinking about the unfortunate victims and what it must have been like for their families.

The dental staff played a minor role the day that Viking went down. However, just a few months before, on the afternoon of Sunday, 24 April 1988, when the submarine USS Bonefish suffered a devastating fire while conducting training exercises with the USS Kennedy (along with the USS Carr and USS McCloy), dental personnel were called upon to play a more involved role.

Because of the fire, the USS Bonefish rapidly filled with thick black smoke and the order was given to abandon ship. Of the ninety-one men aboard, eighty-eight escaped and were picked up by the USS Carr and helicopters from the USS Kennedy. Twenty-two of the rescued men suffered from severe burns and smoke inhalation injuries requiring treatment aboard the carrier. In order to treat this number of victims, the Kennedy activated its mass casualty response team. Dentists and dental assistants were involved in performing triage (determining the severity and extent of injuries and then prioritizing treatment) and CPR. They hooked up IV lines. They administered oxygen, dressed wounds, and monitored and documented vital signs. They helped arrange for food and drink for victims and providers, secured personal effects, and recorded arrival and departure of victims. Since there was no monitoring equipment stored at any of the ship's battle dressing stations, the senior dental officer directed that the Life-Pack 5, Physio-Control ECG, Dinamap electronic blood pressure machine, and Ohmeda pulse oximeter be removed from the oral surgery operatory and moved to the Forward BDS. Ship's electricians then rigged extension cords to provide power for this equipment. The teamwork and strong desire to do one's best certainly helped, as all of the victims who escaped from the submarine were to survive.

And on 23 October 1983, Navy dental personnel also had their daily routine jolted when a terrorist driving a truck loaded with explosives slammed into the lobby of the Marine headquarters and barracks of Battalion 1/8, 24th Marine Amphibious Unit (MAU) at Beirut International Airport. Two-hundred forty-one American servicemen were killed when the resulting explosion leveled the four-story building where several hundred military personnel were asleep. The only medical officer around was killed in the explosion. Two Navy dentists assigned to the 24th MAU were within five-hundred yards of the blast and immediately responded by mustering a group of Navy corpsmen and dental technicians and providing the first emergency treatment to the wounded. The dentists were Lieutenant G.U. Bigelow and Lieutenant J.J. Ware, and the Navy dental technicians were DT3 W. Fly and DN M. Bernal. Lieutenant Bigelow worked with five hospital corpsmen in providing emergency treatment. Lieutenant Ware set up a battalion aid station and, assisted by ten hospital corpsmen and the two dental technicians, performed the initial triage, tagged and identified patients, started intravenous procedures, and provided other emergency care such as splinting, bleeding control, and pain relief. During the first two hours following the explosion, the two dentists and support team treated sixty-five casualties and prepared them for evacuation to treatment ships offshore. At the same time, medical personnel from nearby ships were brought to the disaster site to augment the medical support there.

To my knowledge, everything in this book is true, although some names have been changed. *Snapshot: Ship's Dentists* is not a book filled to the brim with character development and spectacular, entertaining human follies and predicaments. It is instead just a nonchalant description of one person's adventure, told in an unadorned, straightforward manner. The spaces between human beings—their ideas, dreams, desires, divorces, personal tragedies, shortcomings and strengths, and outrageous shenanigans—are not drawn in. That would be for another, different book—one that offers more than just a snapshot.

I put this work together to give back to an organization that is like a big family—maybe the book might stimulate the interest of dental students so perhaps some might consider serving in the Navy. And as it portrays an alternative career path in dentistry, for nonmilitary colleagues it might open up new perspectives on this wonderful profession we share. And it may give people outside the dental occupation a perfunctory peek into navy and dental life. All in all, I hope it makes for an interesting adventure.

PART ONE

INDOCTRINATION

It was in junior year during a recruiter's visit to the dental school that I decided the Navy would be a great way to go. They never had to sell me on anything. I liked what I saw, had a strong sense this was a good deal, and willfully bought the whole idea even though I never considered myself a military type. My hunch proved to be correct as I was to verify years later when reflecting back on the entire experience. What the recruiters said turned out to be true, plus there were many additional benefits they didn't even mention.

Before this, I had never given the armed services much thought. Yeah, I heard news stories about the Navy's role in the attack on Libya in the 1980's. And there were other military incidents that sporadically appeared in the headlines. Several of my uncles served in World War Two and I heard a few brief tales from their adventures. My dad was on a destroyer in the 1950's for two years, but I don't remember him talking much about it. In fact, I never knew he spent time in Newport, Rhode Island until I was preparing to go there for the first destination in my navy career. As a child, I remember reading his *Bluejacket's Manual* (the Navy's handbook for sailors), finding the "abandon ship" instructions on how to ward off sharks very interesting.

Upon graduating from the University of Pittsburgh School of Dental Medicine in the summer of 1986, I was not to report to Officer Indoctrination School (OIS) until January 1987. During the few months between my leaving the city of the Steelers and reporting for active duty, I sold TV's, VCR's, and luggage at a department store in a mall. Fresh out of the dental school curriculum, I caught myself referring to store customers as "patients" on a number of occasions. "I sold two TV's to a couple patients this morning," I reported to my manager, who immediately became engulfed with a puzzled look all over his face.

It was a snowy and frigid January when I packed some things into my new Honda CRX, the first car I ever owned, purchased just three months before, and departed my childhood homeland of Olyphant, Pennsylvania, a small coal mining town about a two hour drive west of New York City. The destination was Newport, Rhode Island, site of OIS. I had a few vague preconceptions, but did not know for sure what to expect there. I had applied to the Navy and Air Force, but throughout the application process felt more at home with the Navy, like I belonged there. However, along the trek to Newport, I wondered what I was doing joining the armed services while fellow graduates from my class were setting up roots, beginning to establish their own private practices. There were several reasons why I decided to sign up.

I was drawn primarily to the opportunity to work in a group practice setting where there could be team interplay among dentists, specialists, and other medical personnel. This would be advantageous to me because, as I wrote in a memo at the time, "I could strengthen and expand the skills and knowledge learned in school" by interacting with other providers. I already felt confident, but wanted to learn even more.

I also wrote, "This group practice concept is also advantageous to patients because it augments their level of health care and thus affects their lives in a more positive way." Patients could have the benefit of having convenient access to an assortment of dental providers who could more easily consult and work with each other and thus, in theory, provide a higher level of quality care.

I was attracted to the reality that the Navy would provide freedom from private practice financial burdens. There was a huge education debt to pay and I did not want to add more to it by buying a dental practice or renting a building, for example.

Having just devoted tremendous amounts of time to the completion of four years of college followed by four more of dental school, I now had a desire to pursue personal goals not related to academia. Figuring out the business aspect of dentistry would require more time and sacrifice. I wanted a balanced lifestyle, with regular work hours. I did not want to take my job home with me, and I had had enough of studying for hours and hours every day.

I liked the idea that joining the Navy would permit me to buy some time so I could defer setting up roots, especially since I was unsure of where I wanted to live. This would be a great opportunity to explore more of the world and settle the question of location without having ties to any particular area.

The benefits were attractive. There were thirty days of paid vacation each year. Medical and dental care was free. There were regular and reasonable work hours. Continuing education opportunities were plentiful. There was a guaranteed income, with salary increases for seniority in length of service and higher rank. There was no need for disability insurance or malpractice insurance. There were tax-free allowances for housing and food. There were retirement benefits. Most bases had excellent recreational facilities. Dental school loans could be deferred for up to three years. There was the social prestige of being a United States Navy officer.

There were opportunities for branching out within the career of dentistry. For example, there was ample room for teaching. Or you could become a specialist or go into research. You could also get into the area of administration.

I had always held a deep fascination with the ocean. Now would be my opportunity to be close to the waves. Growing up in a state without a coastline, it was always a great thrill for me when my parents drove my brothers and me to the Jersey shore for vacations. After leaving the rolling hills of Pennsylvania, the ground gradually got flatter and seagulls began to appear in the sky. It was all very exciting. The most fascinating part was the actual moment when the sea and its endless horizon were first sighted. That had a great impact on me. The world suddenly became larger.

As a child, I collected seaweeds and shells, built sand castles, and dove into the incoming swells. It amazed me that somewhere beneath the water's surface lurked such a variety of fish, crustaceans, and other creatures. Anything having to do with marine biology was fascinating to me. I read the books of Thor Heyerdahl and watched the television shows of Jacques Cousteau. In grade school history class, I thrilled at the tales of the great world explorers such as Vasco da Gama and Magellan. By joining the Navy, I could have a chance to live in more intimate contact with the ocean.

Finally, since my father was a Navy veteran, I would be proud to carry on where he left off. This would be something more the two of us could now have in common. I thought that alone would be something special.

So with all these reasons for joining the Navy, there I was heading to OIS in January of 1987, during a particularly brutal winter season.

Upon reaching Newport, it was fairly easy to find Gate One of the naval base. I stopped, obtained a car pass and, once through the checkpoint, followed the road a short distance to a narrow bridge that passed over a body of water, conveying me to the larger part of the base. A curious, strange system of silver, above-ground ducts lined the waterfront drive, white puffs of steam emanating from it, clouding the visibility as I drove along the roadway. I traversed to Nimitz Hall, where I was to live during the six weeks of OIS.

To check in, coat and tie were required for the men, while "comparable apparel" was required for the women. We reported for duty, gathering in the dormitory. One by one, new faces appeared. By 1600 (4:00 PM) on this sunny Sunday, most of the students had arrived. There were medical doctors, lawyers, dentists, nurses, medical technologists, pharmacists, and hospital administrators. All in all, the entire class size was about seventy people, hailing from different parts of the United States.

I heard someone ask, as if we had just been locked up in a prison, "So what are you in for?" Another person added, "Running from the law?" and everyone laughed. "Come on, you must be running away from something . . ." One woman said she was recently divorced and starting a new life. One of the men indicated he wanted adventure, that he was just trying to escape from his small, boring, landlocked town. Another exclaimed that he just needed a job.

We were divided into groups called *companies*, the individuals of each company destined to work together as a close unit throughout the course. I became part of Golf Company. Lieutenant (LT) Lyons, a salty looking naval officer with thick, curled eyebrows, was assigned as our Company Commander. I thought he looked like a captain of an old whaling ship. We had a *muster*, which was naval talk for a meeting, and the lieutenant introduced us to the Navy. He would direct our group of Staff Corps officers through OIS.

There were two main types of officers in the Navy: *Staff Corps* and *Line*. Line officers were the warriors, ship drivers, pilots and such. Staff Corps officers were the support people like the doctors, dentists, lawyers, and chaplains. OIS was the orientation school for the Staff Corps officers. Some referred to OIS as the "knife and fork school for doctors and lawyers."

LT Lyons was reassuring and put us at ease that first day, but he also warned we had a lot of work to do and the going would get rough at times. We needed to be alert, he instructed, and follow the rules because there would be adverse consequences if we failed to do so.

We were cast into a new culture with rules very foreign to our heretofore way of life, such as the one that said books had to be organized on our shelves from tallest to shortest. I remember thinking, for the life of me, that I could not appreciate the importance of this. I thought to myself, "If Einstein would have worried so much about the proper arrangement of his textbooks, he probably would not have had time to come up with $E=MC^2$."

We were assigned a place to stay. I shared a small, basic room with another dentist. We each had a bed and bedside desk. There was sufficient closet space. My roommate was from somewhere in the Midwest.

There was the morning wakeup—much earlier than most of us were accustomed to—followed by jogging or aerobics, as well as pushups, sit-ups, and other physical fitness training. Afterwards we lined up to take showers prior to breakfast.

Since we did not have enough time to eat breakfast in the mess hall, we supplied our own food and stored it in the community kitchen where we had access to a refrigerator, microwave, and plenty of shelves.

Within the first couple days we went to the barbershop to get haircuts. It was just like in the movies, with everyone lining up to take a turn, copious amounts of hair falling to the floor. Prior to coming to Newport, we were sent an information booklet that instructed us to groom our hair appropriately, but some of the "OISters" apparently did not get the information or did not pay too much attention to it. So the barbering session was the time for the Navy to even off the board. Now we all had hair with that high-and-tight, inspection-ready, tapered-in-the-back look.

We were hustled en masse through the uniform store, fitted swiftly for the wide assortment of uniforms we would need. There was the black coat and tie, black trousers and white epauletted shirt of the Service Dress Blue uniform, the formal uniform that could be worn year-round. There was the "winter blue" uniform, with its black pants and long-sleeved black shirt and tie which we would wear most of the time at OIS. This was the working uniform during the winter months. Someone remarked that it made us look like junior Nazi storm-troopers. During the summer, the working uniform would be either the khaki-colored short-sleeve shirt and pants or the "summer white" uniform with its white short-sleeved shirt and pants. No tie was worn with either of the summer uniforms. For formal occasions, there was the Service Dress White uniform, often called the "choker whites" because the gold-buttoned shirt needed to be fastened tightly all the way up the neck.

We purchased two pairs of black shoes (one pair with the killer shine, the other just a normal shoe), one pair of white shoes, socks, a plain gold tie bar, three different belts (khaki, white, and black), brass belt buckles, a lightweight black jacket, a lightweight khaki jacket, a heavy raincoat, winter gloves, white formal gloves, a garrison cap, an officer's framed cover with gold hat band, a sweatshirt, sweatpants, workout shorts, and several yellow OIS T-shirts. I could never have imagined we'd need all of this apparel.

Our heads were spinning as we progressed through the assembly line of the uniform store. We just had to hope that the ladies taking the body measurements were not mixing up the numbers as they read their tape rulers. Fortunately, as it turned out, for most of us they did a pretty good job.

With all these uniforms came many inspections. A lot of time was spent trying to lift lint off the black cloth of the winter uniforms using sticky materials like masking tape. We also became experts at using Brasso to shine up the belt buckles. The art of shoe shining was perfected as well. We had to pin the various rank and corps devices onto precisely specified locations on the shirts and jackets. All of these things were evaluated closely during the uniform inspections.

The Navy had its own language, filled with acronyms such as AIMD, 3-M PMS and MDS, and phrases like *aye, aye, Sir!* The right side of a ship was called *starboard*, the left, *port*. The place to eat was the *mess hall* for the enlisted personnel and the *wardroom* for officers. *Attention on deck!* was yelled out when a high ranking officer entered a *space*, which was Navy for room. A wall was no longer a wall, but now became a *bulkhead*. A ceiling was the *overhead*, the floor the *deck*. And if you had to go to the bathroom, you had better ask, "Where is the *head*?" *Sir* and *Ma'am* were commonplace designations to be used when speaking to individuals. *Boatswain* was not pronounced as it would appear phonetically, but rather as "bo-sun." Stairs were *ladders*. Nine o'clock in the morning became *zero nine-hundred*, and was written as *0900*. January 24, 1987 became 24 Jan 87. A ship was a "she," and a submarine a *boat*, never to be called a ship. To be assigned to a *duty station* meant that you were *attached* to it.

A hat now was called a *cover* and there was an entire protocol for when and when not to wear a cover. For example, when you were outside, you needed to be "covered," that is, needed to have your cover on. When you entered a private office, you were to uncover.

However, you could remain covered when you walked around inside a public place like a grocery store, bank lobby, or Burger King.

There was a protocol for saluting. For example, Navy personnel only saluted when covered, unlike the Army people who could salute when uncovered. You were to come to attention while saluting except if you were engaged in walking at the time the salute was initiated. We were informed that about six paces was about the proper distance to be away from someone when the salute was to be initiated. The person of the more junior rank was to be the person to initiate. If you were carrying two grandiose bags of groceries and someone passing you saluted, there was no need to drop the bags to the ground in order to return the salute. The rules specified that this was not necessary in a situation like this. When overtaking a senior you would salute and say, "By your leave, Sir?" to which he would respond, "Very well" and return the salute. You could then proceed to pass him. The salute was a form of courtesy, respect, and camaraderie among service personnel.

We learned the names of each Navy rank, from lowest to highest in seniority for officers and enlisted personnel. For officers it was ensign, lieutenant junior grade, lieutenant, lieutenant commander, commander, captain, and then on to admiral. We also learned the equivalent ranks of the other military services, which had different names from Navy. For example, a sergeant in the army was a petty officer second class in the Navy. We also noted that a captain in the Marine Corps was actually much lower in seniority than a captain in the Navy.

There were room inspections. In addition to the obvious requirement of neatness and cleanliness, everything inside our two-man rooms had to be arranged symmetrically, with no deviations. If a briefcase was placed on the right side of a desk on the right side of the room, there needed to be a briefcase located to the left of the desk on the left side—a mirror image.

One day I brought my cross-country skis in from the car. They were just benignly leaning against the closet in my room when it was suddenly announced we were to have an immediate, short-notice room inspection. I really didn't want to drag the bulky skis and poles all the way back to the car out on the frigid windblown parking area nor did I have much time, so I rearranged these so they were bilaterally symmetrical with the layout of the room. I forget exactly where I put them but remember that the creative arrangement brought a grin to the face of the inspector, and my roommate and I passed.

The first two or three days I experienced severe doubts about what I had gotten myself into. It was certainly a different lifestyle from that to which I was accustomed. But, at dinner one evening, I discovered I was not alone, for there were many others who began to divulge their own similar wonderings. It was then that I realized this could actually be fun. I decided to just play this game by the given rules without trying to decipher the rationale behind everything. Also, this new culture began to remind me of Boy Scout experiences, with the uniforms, ranks, badges, inspections, salutes, and other things I had already delved into years ago. And from then on, OIS became a somewhat more enjoyable challenge.

In addition to gaining knowledge about naval customs and etiquette, and how to wear the uniform, salute, speak, and identify rank, there was a great deal of classroom time spent learning other subjects. And much of our after-class time was engaged in studying for the many written tests we were given concerning this material.

One subject studied was Military Law, in which we discussed the reason it was important for the Navy to have its own justice system rather than to use the civilian court system. It was a matter of convenience, for it would be time-consuming, costly, and disruptive of military operations to bring witnesses back to the States from anywhere in the world where the Navy operated.

We talked about the Universal Code of Military Justice (UCMJ), court martial, the difference between criminal and civil law, concurrent jurisdiction, specific and general intent offenses, and the "fruit of the poisoned tree doctrine." We learned how to write up charges and specifications, how to properly search and seize property, and how to apprehend, arrest, and confine. We defined legal jargon such as contraband, pretrial restraint, and probable cause. We learned that, if we decided to run away from OIS, we would be

"UA," or engaging in "Unauthorized Absence." We learned that it was important to avoid "missing ship's movement,"—i.e. ship leaves port for two-week deployment without you because you screwed up—since this could really mess up the Captain's schedule, not to mention the logistics and expense hassles it would create just to get you back to your workplace.

We studied the Law of Armed Conflict, which was a set of principles to be adhered to during time of war. There was one problem: not every nation of the world recognized this. Nevertheless, it represented at least some attempt to limit unnecessary suffering of civilians, prisoners of war, and the wounded, sick or shipwrecked during hostilities among nations. One principle stated that you would only fight combatants, and that you would destroy no more than your mission required. You would not attack civilians and enemy soldiers who surrendered. You would not torture prisoners of war. We learned that medical personnel were classified as noncombatants, their purpose for existing in a theatre of war being for humanitarian purposes and not for engaging directly in armed conflict. In fact, those of us in the medical field had a special Geneva Convention designation inscribed on our military ID cards marking us as medical personnel. We could carry small weapons solely to be used for protecting ourselves and our patients from unlawful attack. All of this impressed on us the serious nature of what it meant to be part of a military organization.

We studied Human Resources Management, which involved programs to help military personnel. The first page of our notes on this subject addressed the U.S. Department of Defense's "Human Goals." The text began with the following: "Our nation was founded on the principle that the individual has infinite dignity and worth. The Department of Defense, which exists to keep the nation secure and at peace, must always be guided by this principle. In all that we do, we must show respect for the serviceman, servicewoman and the civilian employee, recognizing their individual needs, aspirations and capabilities." This being said, Human Resources Management involved the attempt to live up to these words, taking the form of various programs designed to help personnel. I was very impressed with the emphasis the Navy gave to this subject.

There was the Equal Opportunity Policy, which set out to ensure that personnel, regardless of race, creed, sex, or national origin, received equal treatment and had equal opportunity, that the factors which affected individual promotion, training, assignment to duty, and any other action would be based upon merit, ability, performance and potential. We discussed at great length the efforts that would be undertaken to try to make this happen, such as the formation of Command Training Teams that would conduct workshops on a regular basis. We reviewed grievance procedures, which served to guide an individual in the event that problems were encountered.

There was the Sexual Harassment Policy, the Alcohol and Drug Abuse Program, and the Waste, Fraud and Abuse Abatement System. The latter intended to provide an easy means by which anyone could report deficiencies in policy or material to a central agency, which would then investigate further to eliminate misguided policies or actions such as the renowned purchase of thousand-dollar toilet seats.

There was the Family Advocacy Program which addressed child/ spouse maltreatment, sexual assault and rape. It involved prevention, identification, intervention, and treatment.

There was the Overseas Duty Support Program which aimed to improve individual and family experience in a host country's unique environment, promoting positive relations between the Navy and countries in which the Navy operated.

And since we were now government employees, we had to understand government ethics and follow certain standards of conduct. For example, we could not use rank, title, or position for commercial purposes, and there were rules governing the giving of gifts to superiors and the accepting of gifts from subordinates.

All of these programs were part of the Human Resources Management curriculum at OIS.

I think it was during the third week that we received immunizations for yellow fever and other such exotic diseases we could contract if sent to certain areas of the world. We were told that, because of the immunizations, we had to be quarantined on the base for a couple weeks, so we had to spend a few weekends without going into town. One OIS student lamented, "Now we're all stuck together with each other with no place to go," to which another added, "Yeah, kinda' like how it must be aboard a ship, eh?"

To pass the time during the quarantine, many movies were watched in the dorm TV room on the VCR. There was *Officer and a Gentleman* and other navy films in the collection. They had a piano there, on which someone attempted to play *Anchors Away*. Some nonsmokers actually took up smoking because "it was just something to do." We also played volleyball and racquetball at the gym. I had a double-cassette tape recorder with me and, at the request of one of the physical fitness instructors, spent some spare time putting together a compilation of music on cassette tapes to be used during the early morning running and aerobics training.

We lived for lunch. It was something to look forward to, our social hour. Often during morning classes you would see the Menu of the Day passed around by the students, and you'd see eyes light up with joy in anticipation of the upcoming meal.

I visited the USS Simpson, a destroyer anchored at the pier. It was the first time I boarded a Navy ship, its grey color and sturdy metal frame presenting what looked like an ominous and uncomfortable habitat for its sailors.

As I said, it was a harsh winter. The base actually had to close down twice during our stay because of the severe blizzards that passed through. LT Lyons said to see a base close was a rare event. I recall deep snow drifts and twisted and bent stop signs nearly knocked over from the high winds.

I hiked around the base on a few occasions and remember stopping at the end of the long pier near Nimitz Hall to gaze out over the water, trying to contemplate how those sturdy, rugged seagulls could thrive in such cold conditions. I dreamed about the hot summer sun and sand of Virginia Beach that lay awaiting me after I would depart OIS and New England to head south to my next duty station in Norfolk. The thought warmed me as I gazed out over the frigid Narragansett Bay.

In our orientation to the Navy, we looked at naval history. Names like John Paul Jones, Stephen Decatur, Isaac Hull, Oliver Hazard Perry, David Farragut, George Dewey, Robert E. Peary, and Chester Nimitz were evoked from the pages of the history books. Vessels such as "Old Ironsides," the Monitor and Merrimack—and don't forget the Maine—sailed again. Famous quotes such as "Don't give up the ship!" and "Damn the torpedoes! Full speed ahead!" and "I have not yet begun to fight!" were restated.

In the subject of Administration and Career Development, we learned some of the fringe benefits to which naval personnel and their dependents were entitled. One of these benefits was shopping privileges or access to the following facilities found on most bases: Navy Exchange (department store, general store), commissary (grocery), Mini-Mart (convenience store), gas station, automobile service station, post office, bank, laundry, dry cleaning facility, package store (liquor store), dental and medical clinics, legal aid office, MWR (Morale, Welfare and Recreation Office), theatre, and chapel.

We talked about the different types of orders we could receive, the most common being PCS orders (Permanent Change of Station), which involved *detachment*, another new term, from one duty station to another. A *duty station* was where you were assigned to work. When they said "permanent," they meant long-term, perhaps three to five years, before you would have to move on to a new duty station. PCS orders were the civilian equivalent of an employee getting a job transfer within the same company, moving from one office in California to another in New York City, for example.

If the orders we received said "You are hereby detached within twenty-four hours," it meant we needed to move all our possessions within twenty-four hours. This order was not too common, however, except that it could be found sometimes during war.

You could also receive temporary orders, which I would see during subsequent years when I would leave work at a dental clinic to attend continuing education for a few days somewhere where travel was involved, for example to Bethesda, Maryland, home of the Navy's dental school.

We learned to calculate Travel Time, which was time allotted an individual in moving to a new duty station, not to be deducted from his accumulated leave days.

We learned that once every year we would be filling out Officer Preference and Personal Information Cards, otherwise known as "Dream Sheets." It was interesting to me that we had some freedom to actually request specific duty stations and that somewhere there was an individual called the *detailer* who would try, some more so than others, to grant your wishes when it came time to move on. Of course, despite your desires, in the end it would be the "needs of the Navy" that would ultimately determine where you would indeed end up. You basically had to be flexible. But I must say during my time on active duty, I was able to observe a good effort put forth by the detailers to grant our wishes, certainly mine.

We discussed shipping our personal property from one place to another. They had it all figured out. You would first contact the expert, the Personal Property Office, who would fill you in on details such as how much total weight of goods you would be allotted to have shipped at government expense. They would tell you that live plants, perishable items, alcoholic beverages, aerosol cans, flammables and acids were not authorized for shipment. They would tell you that you needed seven copies of your orders to make the move happen. I would learn that, in the modern Navy, the copy machine was essential. Over the years, I found myself making copies of everything. I don't know how they functioned without this in the days of John Paul Jones.

We learned how to figure out our pay (taxable income) and allowances (non-taxable income). Base Pay was the main type of taxable income and was based on number of years in service and rank. BAQ (Basic Allowance for Quarters) was a set amount of money we would be paid to cover costs of housing. VHA (Variable Housing Allowance) was begun in 1980 to give service people more tax-free money for housing, the amount tailored to meet costs (which of course varied in different areas of the United States) above that which was covered by BAQ. BAS (Basic Allowance for Subsistence) was a set amount of money we would be paid to cover costs of meals. Per Diem was allowances authorized to defray the cost of meals and lodging incurred during travel.

We practiced writing performance evaluations for workers under our command. These reports were called *Fitreps* (Fitness Reports) for officers and *Evals* for enlisted. In addition, we were exposed to the various forms of naval correspondence, which could appear as *instructions* (to establish long-term policy), *notices* (to establish short-term policy), or *memorandums* (informal messages).

All the topics mentioned above were included as part of the Administration and Career Development curriculum.

We also spent considerable time looking at Leadership, Management Education and Training (LMET). This was a review of the basic principles underlying effective leadership and personnel management. We studied command climate and the various leadership styles, as well as team building, for example.

Outside of the classroom were other projects and requirements to fulfill. Twice we went to the pool. The first time was to take the swimming test, which included jumping off a ten-foot tower, treading water for five minutes, and swimming fifty yards. The second visit to the pool included jumping into the water with clothes on, then inflating the clothes to serve as life preservers. All of these represented skills that could possibly be needed for survival if the call to abandon ship was issued some interesting day. You just never would know when you might have to jump from the deck of a ship into the deep ocean, and then have to find some way to stay afloat, awaiting rescue.

One person from our company could not get herself to do the tower jump because she was so terrified, so the staff had to work with her on many additional days until she was able to do it. Our company really came together to urge her on, and everyone was so happy when she conquered this obstacle.

We spent a large amount of time *drilling*, which meant marching. We were given instructions in standard military formations and the basic maneuvers of close order drill. We learned moves like "Right

Face," "About Face," and "Halt." We could maneuver straight ahead as a group, at oblique angles, in circles, all over. Whenever OIS students travelled by foot on base in groups of two or more, they had to march. So from time to time you would see several small groups of people marching along the sidewalks and fields of the base.

Whenever our whole company moved from a classroom in one building to another building, we marched, and the Company Duty Officer (CDO) of the day—someone from our group; we took turns—called out the commands. One time, there was a pretty girl in civilian clothes walking ahead and to the right of the group, approaching us. Of course, the guys could not help but notice her. When she was to our right and soon to pass us, our perceptive CDO called out "Eyes, Right!" so we could turn our heads to the right while continuing to march forward, allowing us to look at her a little longer before she faded out of sight.

We visited the dental clinic to get our first Navy checkup. Navy personnel were required to have an initial dental workup followed by subsequent annual exams, called a *T2 exam*, which comprised a comprehensive hard and soft tissue evaluation that included an oral cancer screening exam (OCSE) and use of the mouth mirror, periodontal probe, and appropriate x-rays as needed. It also included a blood pressure recording and health questionnaire review. At OIS, an initial charting of existing dental restorations and conditions was compiled, thus completing the construction of our official dental charts, which would be carried along with us thenceforth wherever new duty stations took us.

We had to accumulate thirty-five aerobic points a week while at OIS, and had to pass a physical fitness test that involved pushups, sit-ups, pull-ups, and a one and a half mile run.

We were introduced to Damage Control, which involved procedures necessary to the survival of a ship following damage acquired from bomb explosions, collisions, or any other destructive enemy contact with the ship. Damage control involved fire-fighting, restoring damaged piping systems, making the ship watertight and airtight, maintaining reserve buoyancy and stability, and carrying out decontamination procedures in the event of radiation exposure. Any rupture, break, or hole in the ship's outer hull plating, particularly below the waterline, could let in sea water. If flooding was not controlled, the ship could sink. So in order to remain afloat, you had to either plug the holes or establish and maintain flood boundaries within the ship and thus prevent more extensive flooding. To plug the holes you either had to put something in the hole or over it.

Damage control equipment was stowed in *repair lockers*. The equipment included patches for ruptured water or steam lines, plugs made of soft wood for stopping the flow of liquids in a damaged hull or in broken lines, wooden beams for shoring (a shore was a portable beam or such to brace an object that could become loose, like a hatch or bulkhead), and tools such as axes, crowbars, wrecking bars, and hacksaws. Other kinds of patches included rags, pillows, mattresses, metal plates, and flexible sheet metal plating. Other basic materials included wedges, sholes, and strongbacks.

Armed with this knowledge, one day we marched in the pouring rain for what seemed quite a distance to the USS Buttercup, the simulator that demonstrated very realistically what conditions would be like if water began flooding a ship's compartments. It was another awakening to the serious game into which we had joined.

One by one, our company personnel climbed down the ladder into the spaces below the upper deck of the Buttercup. The scenario to be played out was that our ship had been struck by enemy bombs that ripped through the hull. The lights went out. Saltwater began spraying and gushing all around. As we groped in the dark, trying to work together to repair the damage, the water level gradually rose past knee-level. Cold water pelted our faces as we moved through various areas to mobilize available tools and patches. It was difficult to see. As soon as we plugged one leak, another would appear. We were trapped in the enclosed space like sailors had been in time of war. As the sea level climbed higher, we struggled further. Eventually we finally succeeded in stopping its further flow. We crawled out of the ship, more appreciative of what needed to be done in situations like this.

We learned the types of fires and how to extinguish each. We watched *Trial by Fire*, actual black and white film footage of a fire aboard the USS Forrestal on July 29, 1967 during the Vietnam War. A Zuni rocket was fired accidentally, igniting an A-4 Skyhawk attack jet. Within minutes the ship was in flames. Pilot John McCain, a future U.S. Senator and presidential candidate, managed to narrowly escape death by jumping from his parked aircraft onto the turbulent flight deck where he scurried off to safety. A camera captured the ensuing attempts by crewmen to extinguish the conflagration. As the fire spread, more bombs and other ammunition ignited and exploded. You could see and hear one firefighting party after another get blown up, eerily disappearing from the flight deck and the movie camera's lens as the next group of men moved in. That day, one-hundred thirty-four sailors perished and one-hundred sixty-four more were injured. Following the screening of this footage, we discussed the tragic mishap and explored what might have been done to prevent it. This nightmare film remains etched in my mind to this day.

While at OIS, we engaged in Olympic Games, pitting company against company. Our company named our team Lyons' Lobsters, using one of those plastic lobster bibs you get at seafood restaurants as our official banner. Morale was generally very high in our group throughout our tenure at OIS, including during the Olympic competition.

We were to be photographed in our dress blue uniforms. As I was on my way to get this photo taken, I found myself taking a wrong turn somewhere down an unfamiliar passageway. Upon opening the door of a room at the end of the passageway, I entered and nearly had a heart attack when about seven junior personnel jumped up out of their chairs as one of them yelled out crisply and loudly "Attention on deck!" After regaining my senses and realizing they were just observing another naval custom, I remembered to respond, "Very well." I realized I was not at the photo shoot, so I turned smartly around and exited.

A ship always had sailors *on watch* in order to keep an eye out for the safety of the vessel and its crew. For OIS, the passageways and spaces of the dormitory served as our ship. We took turns at watch standing, ensuring that the logbook was properly inscribed and only authorized personnel entered our assigned zone of responsibility.

We learned what it meant to *swab the deck*. We typically did this during *field days*. The decks were swept, swabbed, and waxed. Field day was cleaning time, when "all hands turned to" and thoroughly cleaned the OIS dormitory spaces and passageways in preparation for an inspection by the Company Commander.

After the quarantine ended, we were allowed to leave the Naval Base and go into town. With the downtown streets and sidewalks covered with snow, icicles hanging from the edges of roofs, and more snowflakes descending, adding to the white covering, Newport was reminiscent of a delightful, peaceful seaside New England village. Evidence of its kinship with the sea was rampantly evident. Seafood restaurants and tattoo parlors abounded. Scrimshaw and crafts from the sea were displayed at various shops. Everywhere were buoys and fishing nets. Icy cold winds blew across the wharves, the bells on the yachts clanging rhythmically.

From its beginnings in 1639, Newport was a haven for pirates and a major port for the profitable slave trade. It was also a big-time center for the trade of molasses and the rum that was made from it. As a busy seaport, it even surpassed New York and Boston at the time. The first naval battle of the American Revolution took place off adjacent Jamestown when the sloop "Katy" captured the Royal Naval sloop "Diana."

In the 1800's the unspoiled beauty and relative isolation of the island was recognized by the wealthy, who began building the enormous homes they called "summer cottages." In an effort to outdo one another, great ornate mansions emerged.

At a restaurant that granted significant discounts to Navy personnel in uniform, I ate lobster for the first time in my life. A group of us from OIS filled an entire large dining table. After dinner, on the way back to our cars while walking along bedecked in our black uniforms, a sports car filled with teenagers flew by and someone menacingly yelled "Squids!" at us. This was a nickname given to Navy sailors. One member of our party was appalled and could not believe anyone would yell such a thing at us who, as he declared, "represent defenders of the United States." I just laughed and shrugged it off because adolescents, especially Americans, were notorious for rebelling against any kind of authority, especially anyone in a uniform.

On another weekend, I drove with my roommate up to Boston. We visited, among other landmarks, the USS Constitution, the oldest commissioned warship afloat in the world. Launched in 1797, she had thirty twenty-four pounder long guns on her gun deck, with shot that could pierce twenty inches of wood at one-thousand yards. The crew was composed of between four to five-hundred men who slept on hammocks.

In those days there was a daily ration of rum or whiskey served from the grog tub. In modern days, the only alcohol aboard ship was contraband or the wine in the chapel, or the cans of beer reserved for extensive periods at sea during which each sailor would be authorized one can.

The USS Constitution had a sick bay, where injured or sick personnel could be medically treated. There were three large installed kettles in which food was cooked. Up above, on each mast, was a "fighting top," from where Marine snipers fired at enemy ship personnel.

At the completion of Officer Indoctrination School, we had a dinner at the Officer's Club and a graduation ceremony in which we displayed our drilling abilities. In later years I would realize on several occasions that the knowledge garnered at OIS gave us distinct advantages: we were introduced to a unique nautical/military culture; we were sufficiently prepared to navigate a naval career and ready to handle positions of greater responsibility. Immediately following the graduation ceremonies, we departed to duty stations all over the world. Most of my OIS comrades I would never see again. I think we were all exhausted from the work we had to do in this boot camp experience. When I drove off the base to head south, there was a feeling of intense relief, like the weight of the world had been removed from my shoulders.

PART TWO

NAVAL DENTAL CENTER

Ninety-degree heat. Blinding sun radiating down, piercing through a perfectly blue sky. Beautiful girls lying out on hot fluffy sand. A refreshingly cool ocean with its constant swells and whitecaps roaring and rolling in toward shore. The smell of sunscreen. Boats on the horizon. To live at the beach was my dream.

Upon returning triumphantly and several pounds lighter from OIS, I stayed a few days at home before proceeding to Norfolk and Virginia Beach in a heavy snowstorm that gradually tapered off the farther south I drove. Somewhere in Delaware the precipitation stopped and soon there was no snow at all blanketing the ground. The change in the weather was a good sign I was getting closer to my dream of living at a summery beach.

Eventually I arrived at the Chesapeake Bay Bridge-Tunnel and was surprised by the pricey nine-dollar toll, initially failing to realize this was not an ordinary bridge. I could never have imagined what the next seventeen miles on this amazing structure would be like. The extremely narrow, two-laned road was elevated high above the crashing waves on a platform that took three-and-a-half years to build, including the two underwater tunnels. Seagulls hovered to the left and right, sometimes close by at eye level. From the middle of the bridge, no land could be seen. You were just surrounded by a desolate ocean wilderness, suspended in the air where you could feel the wind push your vehicle. And the ride took a long time. It was like being out to sea in your car. This was my introduction to Virginia Beach. I would later live near this structure. And in time I would live on another engineering masterpiece, an aircraft carrier.

After finally reaching the end of the bridge, I headed toward Norfolk, the site of the largest naval base in the world. I checked in to the Navy Lodge on Hampton Boulevard, which would be home until more permanent accommodations could be arranged.

The next morning, I reported to Branch Dental Clinic, Naval Base, Norfolk, Virginia. This was the parent command to numerous branch clinics scattered throughout the region in places such as Little Creek, Dam Neck, Portsmouth, Oceana, Yorktown, and Newport News. It was also called Sewell's Point Dental Clinic or "the Big House," and was located just outside the gates of Naval Base Norfolk. In later years, it became known as the Naval Dental Center. I often heard people declare it to be the Navy's largest dental clinic. There must have been at least about thirty specialists and general dentists working at the Naval Dental Center Norfolk, with many more in the branches, perhaps totaling around one-hundred overall.

I was oriented to the facility, given a supply of yellow, zippered smocks, and assigned a locker. We were to wear the uniform of the day—most of the time the khakis—while driving to and from work each day. Upon arriving for work to treat patients, we would simply remove the short-sleeved khaki shirt and put on a smock, keeping on the khaki pants, plain white tee shirt, and black shoes of the uniform. Scrubs had not yet come into vogue as they would in later years.

Escorted into the administrative center, I was introduced to the Commanding Officer, Captain R.A. Webster, who asked a few questions and welcomed me. He said to "Remember that you are an officer first, and a dentist second." This seemed odd, since I considered myself the reverse. More on that later.

I began treating patients the very first day I checked in, working in the Operative Department where I would be for the next four months. This was where basic *dental restorations* (fillings) were done. There was ample time to become familiar with the equipment, supplies, and *dental operating rooms* (DOR), and meet the support staff.

I worked alongside about five or six other dentists, doing *amalgams* (silver fillings) and *composites* (plastic white fillings). Composites were used for *anterior* (front) teeth since their color could blend in so you could not easily tell a dental restoration had been placed. Since amalgams were stronger and more durable, the Navy's policy was to use these routinely for *posterior* (back) teeth, where esthetics would not matter so much. I remember a Navy reservist from New England appeared one day to do his required annual two weeks of active duty. He brought his own state-of-the-art composite materials and began placing posterior composites. Of course this was frowned upon and, when word got around, he was ordered to stop this practice. In later years, as these materials were improved, they would become more acceptable.

Flexible transparent matrices, sandpaper strips, and various finishing burs and disks were used when working with composites. A variety of composite brands was available to us, such as Silux, Prisma, and Heliomolar. Having access to an assortment of materials presented an invaluable opportunity to compare the quality of different products.

We learned to do amazing things with amalgam. When a tooth was severely broken-down, it was often better to have a *crown* ("cap") made by a dental lab because of the resultant enhanced ability to hold the tooth together. But in the military, with restricted public funds and only so many dentists and dental lab technicians to do the work, it was not always possible to fabricate crowns. The standard line throughout the Navy was "It would be nice if you could get a crown on that tooth, but we can't do it here because of the long waiting list. You could see if they would be able to do it at your next duty station." So extremely large amalgams were routinely constructed using retention strategies such as slots, grooves, undercuts, and metal pins to successfully lock the fillings into the teeth and minimize the chance they would dislodge. Many of these amalgams were works of art that held up very well, serving the patient for years. Of course there were other factors to be considered in determining who was eligible for a crown, such as the patient's ability to take care of it by practicing good daily oral hygiene. You would not want to go through all the work and expense required to put a crown on a tooth if a patient was going to let the tooth become carious within the next year; all that effort would be for nothing.

The four-month stint in Operative was an opportunity to get routines down, increase speed and overall quality, and sort through all the various hand instruments to determine which ones were really needed and which were not. I discovered that some instruments had several names, such as one which could be called a "½-1" or a "Hollenbeck carver," and another that was a Tanner carver, a 5-T, or a discoid-cleoid. One time I asked an assistant for a 5-T and he looked at me totally confused and asked, "What's that, Sir? I don't think we have any of those." When I looked through the set of instruments and pointed to it, he said, "Oh, you mean the Tanner?" So we had to name our tools so we'd be on the same page.

It was refreshing to discuss the subtleties of operative dentistry with other dentists, young and old, as this had the effect of augmenting our knowledge and building confidence. For example, the gingival margin trimmer was a nice tool to smooth ragged edges before the filling was packed into the tooth preparation. In dental school, I had always heard students scoff at its use, that it was a waste of time. Yeah, you didn't have to use it for every tooth prep, but it sometimes did have its place in eliminating rough edges that, if left alone, could chip in the future, inviting premature leakage and failure of the restoration. In talking with other dentists here, I found them commending the benefits of this instrument in certain circumstances, and that reinforced my own thoughts about this. This happened with other ideas, too.

This was a time to establish strategies for placing *bases*, which were softer materials applied under restorations to serve as insulation against thermal stimuli (to minimize a tooth's sensitivity to cold or hot) or to induce the tooth to regenerate itself by thickening in the deepest areas. During the course of performing so much operative treatment, I would find occasion to make helpful observations of things such as year-old amalgams breaking in the area where some dentist had placed excessively thick base, thereby weakening the restoration and inviting failure. I had the opportunity to develop specific philosophies for placing bases so they would not jeopardize the durability of a restoration. So we had time to focus on the little things like this.

We were urged to use the *rubber dam* routinely. This was that useful device invented sometime in the 1800's to isolate the area around the teeth to be worked on. Once you installed the rubber dam on your patient, it kept the tongue out of the way, maintained a dry work area, made it easier to see, and prevented debris from getting blown into the patient's throat.

Sometimes we used the automatrix, a contraption I had never seen before, which was helpful for building up severely broken-down teeth that did not present much tooth structure on which to fasten a conventional matrix band and retainer. A matrix was needed to provide a rigid, nonyielding surface against which to pack the relatively soft amalgam before it hardened. This worked much the same way as the wooden forms temporarily erected when concrete was poured.

After having battled through four years of the rigorous and cumbersome dental school setting—appropriate to a certain degree for a school program—with its demand for incessant procedure checks by instructors, I was relieved to discover this new environment to be a refreshing breath of fresh air. The atmosphere was now a more dignified one, where the doctors were treated with respect and trusted for their expertise. There was a noticeable absence of others looking over shoulders as dentistry was practiced. And the equipment was very modern and clean, and rarely broke down.

With this trust came the responsibility to ask questions when they arose, so that the patient would receive the best care possible under all circumstances. If we needed something, we just requested it and usually got it. Also, most of the time, the department coordinator was available to assist with questions or technical problems.

If *caries* (tooth decay) spread into the *pulp* (the hollow center of a tooth that is filled with nerves and blood vessels), the tooth underwent an irreversible inflammatory reaction (we say it would "die") and the patient could experience severe pain and/or swelling at any time. If the perforation into the pulp was small and there were other fortuitous circumstances surrounding the overall situation, there were rare times when the tooth might be all right. But most times, the tooth needed to be extracted (removed) or have root canal therapy.

In the course of treatment in Operative, if a tooth was found to require root canal therapy, we performed a *partial pulpectomy*, a procedure to clean out a substantial portion of the pulp so that the chance of the tooth abscessing over the next couple months was diminished. This would buy time for the patient to schedule as soon as possible a more time-consuming appointment to have the entire pulp cleaned out and filled with a rubbery substance called gutta percha. Ninety-five percent of the time, root canal therapy worked and you were able to save an otherwise hopeless tooth.

Later, when I would practice civilian dentistry, the treatment I would perform for these situations would be very different. For example, there was no need to remove so much of the pulp during that first visit, especially when it could be more difficult to numb up one-hundred percent. But in the military, the approach had to be different, more aggressive, since there was no way to know if a patient would be summoned to a theatre of war the next day or before the root canals could be sealed fully. Until they were sealed, there remained the risk that an acute abscess could present. And if you did not remove as much of the pulp as a partial pulpectomy achieved, there was a greater chance the tooth could flare up. If it then became abscessed during some combat mission, for example, the military operation could be jeopardized if one of the essential players suffered down time due to a severe toothache. We had to think ahead about unexpected contingencies. So that was the reason a greater part of the pulp had to be cleaned out on active duty patients. And it was also an example of one of the differences between military and civilian dentistry.

We reported for work at 0645 Monday through Friday and began seeing patients at 0700. It soon became obvious, however, that the better thing to do was to show up earlier so you could gather around

Captain Whitaker's desk to listen to his sea stories. Here was a tall old salty veteran, the Head of the Operative Department, who knew how to tell a tale. He was a practical man. I recall one time when I was sent to take a one-week course on Leadership Management Education Training (LMET), an exceptional program said to have the same curriculum that corporate individuals pay over a thousand dollars each to take. It involved didactic material but also a great degree of hands-on practical training. When I returned to the Big House after being away attending this course, Captain Whitaker half-jokingly said with a grin, "Now that you learned all of that, you could forget it all because here's how things actually work . . ." He then proceeded to relay the wisdom of his vast experiences in the real world.

Some patients had appointments, while others just checked in to the clinic and sat in the waiting room until there was an appointment space available. Some days, the latter might hang around all day and not be seen for lack of available space.

Patients were from all over the United States. We got to hear a variety of dialects and accents. Many of the patients were attached to shore commands, but many were from ships. The only types of Navy ships that had their own dentists aboard were aircraft carriers, battleships, tenders, and Marine amphibious ships, for the most part. All the others, like destroyers and cruisers, had to rely on shore commands such as our clinic to provide dental services. So I treated patients from ships such as the USS Dahlgren and USS Coontz (guided missile destroyers), the USS Peterson and USS Comte De Grasse (destroyers), the USS Milwaukee (oiler), the USS Bainbridge (nuclear-powered missile cruiser), the USS Belknap and USS Harry E. Yarnell (guided missile cruisers), and the USS Elmer Montgomery and USS Aylwin (frigates).

Some patients were from foreign countries. Norfolk was a busy naval base, often visited by NATO ships. I remember treating sailors from the Royal Navy and the Portuguese Navy. To communicate with the non-English speaking sailors, I often found myself drawing pictures on the bracket table paper or using exaggerated hand gestures. We discovered international symbols for "Where does it hurt?" and "Are you okay?" or "How ya doooin'?"

Occasionally, we treated patients from other branches of the service. Army dental charts had paperwork right-side-up on the left side and upside-down on the right, supposedly to facilitate stacking of charts; they would be flatter since one flexible metal fastener was located at the top of the left side, while the fastener for the right side was found at the right bottom, and they would not oppose each other when the chart was closed and inserted into a row of other charts on a shelf.

Air Force charts were distinguished by their typed-out case notes, as opposed to the handwritten ones everyone else produced. And it seemed, from what I observed, that Air Force dentists relished the use of multiple pins for retention of large dental restorations. When I looked at an x-ray of a tooth that had five pins showing up, I could bet money it was done by Air Force.

Some retirees showed up almost every day for treatment on a space-available basis. Many of them had those large amalgams I previously described, still holding up well. Periodically they would require patches where the amalgam had chipped or where there was recurrent caries. I heard some great sea tales from them while we waited for the anesthesia to take effect, and sometimes wondered if half of it was stretched a little.

Navy dentistry presented interesting situations each day. One time a patient who resided in the *brig* (naval jail) was escorted to the dental clinic in chains by armed guards. He was a huge guy complaining of a toothache. His arms and ankles were bound throughout his appointment. Don't know what offense he committed to get to jail. While he underwent dental treatment, a couple times he had to scratch his itchy nose, chains rattling as he struggled to carry out this maneuver.

If you had a Navy SEAL in your chair as a patient, you had better be flexible and ready to alter your dental treatment plan because he might be called away at any time to some special mission. I was at a friend's party one night and two of his neighbors, both SEALs, were there having a good time. All of a sudden their beepers went off and they had to step out to a place where they could have privacy. They were gone for a while and when they returned, one held out his hand as if trying to calm everybody down and said, "It's okay. America is safe. Carry on." Navy SEALs would sometimes get called up and disappear for weeks at a time, and they couldn't tell anyone where they were.

Inside each patient's Navy chart were *progress notes*. At the top of every page of the progress notes were two boxes, each with a small drawing of thirty-two teeth. During a dental exam, pathologies were drawn in pencil on the appropriate tooth in the right-hand box. The pencil entry served as a worksheet and a quick way to identify what needed to be done. When the pathology was treated, the pencil mark was erased and the restoration or other treatment was indicated in black ink in the left-hand box. This system was useful when scanning through pages of a patient's dental history to find all entries relating to a particular tooth.

Charts were tagged as being *class one, two, three,* or *four.* Class one meant the patient had no pathologies. Class two meant there were minor pathologies like gingivitis or incipient caries that would not cause a dental emergency within the next year when the person might be away at sea or deployed with the Marines, for example, in a place isolated from care. Class three meant there were pathologies present that were likely to cause a dental emergency within the next year, conditions such as caries, impacted third molars with history of pericoronitis, moderate and advanced periodontitis, and chronic apical periodontitis secondary to irreversible pulpitis. Class four meant the person was overdue for his required annual T2 exam.

According to U.S. Navy training manuals, the mission of the United States Armed Forces is **to prepare and conduct prompt and sustained combat operations in support of the national interest.** And regarding us in the Navy Dental Corps, what it all came down to was that our primary mission was to help prevent or correct disabilities that could hinder armed forces personnel in their ability to prepare and conduct prompt and sustained combat operations in support of the national interest. That was the way I saw it. *Dental readiness* was the measurement of how well the Dental

Corps was doing in achieving that mission. If a ship had 85% of its crew at class one or two, then its dental readiness was 85%. But this also meant that 15% of the crew was class three or four and needed either T2 exams or corrective treatment to get out of the unacceptable categories. Dental readiness was really our small, but essential, niche in the overall mission of the Navy. It was the Navy Dental Corps' reason for being.

When we finished a patient's treatment plan, we also performed a thorough dental exam to ensure there was nothing new to be done. Then the patient would be due for another exam in exactly one year from the date of that exam.

There were great benefits to be found by any person just out of dental school working for months in the Operative Department, doing the same types of restorations each day, but there was also the disadvantage that, after a while, the work had a tendency for some individuals to approach drudgery. Somebody referred to it as the "Amalgam Line" and wrote words to be sung to Johnny Cash's *I Work the Line*. This frustrated soul wrote:

> I keep a close watch on this tech of mine.
> I keep my fluoride ready all the time.
> I keep my fillings burnished so they shine.
> I'm talkin' about the amalgam line.
> Yeah, I'm talkin' about the amalgam line.
> I keep my DIRS forms filled out properly.
> I keep my carbon paper with me constantly.
> I know Chief Hilton will want to see me,
> 'Cause there ain't no code for a WFT.
> When you're on the line, the amalgam line.
> When you work the line, the amalgam line.
> Well, it's four o'clock on Friday afternoon.
> And I'm thinkin' I'll be leavin' pretty soon.
> Just then an ORF walks in with number 2
> All broken down. What do you do?
> When you're on the line, the amalgam line.
> When you work the line, the amalgam line.

I know it's very, very easy to burn out.
When you work hard and you don't have any clout.
Just keep your mind on retention and box form
And you're guaranteed your daily norm.
When you're on the line, the amalgam line.
When you work the line, the amalgam line.

That was a raw ditty I stumbled upon while at the Big House. I don't remember if I found it scrawled on some bathroom wall or if some desperate soul, in an obvious cry for help, passed out copies to us. A little further investigation reveals that "ORF" refers to an "old retired fellow" or something like that. And it is interesting to note that the extent and location of dental restorations are described by what surfaces of a tooth are involved; for example, an MOD restoration encompasses the mesial, occlusal, and distal surfaces of a tooth. Some fillings were smaller, like an occlusal (O) amalgam, involving only one surface. In comparison, an MODB amalgam was a relatively large restoration. A "WFT" was even bigger; it stood for "the whole fu#$ing thing."

Following dental appointments, each procedure accomplished on a patient was tallied on the DIRS (Dental Information Retrieval System). This was a gauge of our production. The DIRS contained the patient's name, rank, duty station, social security number, and the specific procedures that were done. We also had to denote if the patient was active duty, retired, dependent, etc. It struck me as amusing that we had to claim minor procedures that were actually just parts of larger ones; for example, every time we placed a calcium hydroxide base, we had to tally the number code for "base"; or when cavity varnish was applied, we had to take credit for code 09630 (therapeutic medicaments). There also was a code for cleaning up after the patient. Each code was weighted for a certain amount of points, and these were used to figure out production. For example, a one-surface amalgam was worth 1.0 CTV's (composite time values) while a four-surface amalgam was good for 2.6. Molar root canal therapy counted for 4.4 CTV's if there were four or more canals.

In dental school, we worked mostly alone without an assistant. Now we had assistants assigned to us, and so this presented an opportunity to figure out how to utilize the extra set of hands to increase efficiency. During the first couple weeks in Operative, I was assigned a variety of different assistants, called *dental technicians* in the Navy. Eventually, DN Hansen, a young, single parent, became my permanent tech. *DN* was the Navy's abbreviation for the rank of *Dentalman*. In communicating with our assistants, we would refer to them by their rank and last name.

Unfortunately, DN Hansen proved to be difficult to work with. She was slow in learning my way of doing things and it seemed like every day she constantly complained about how she did not want to work. One time, I asked her if she measured out equal quantities of IRM powder and liquid like I taught her. She said yes, but I doubt it because there was way too much powder on the glass mixing slab.

One day, we finished treating our last scheduled patient of the day and had time to see another patient. DN Hansen cleaned up the room and I instructed her to get a space-available patient from the upstairs waiting room. She did not want to get another patient because she claimed "There are no more of our instrument packs available." I said I would borrow a pack or check with the Central Sterilization Room (CSR) to see if they could have one of our packs ready. I said I'd be right back and went upstairs to get a patient. She disregarded what I said and put everything away and had the chair and trays folded for the weekend. I went to the CSR and easily obtained two of our packs. When I returned to our room, I got our patient seated and started checking the patient's chart. She walked in and slammed something down on the countertop. I could tell that she was mad that I got another patient.

Another time, we had a no-show, and so I told her to check upstairs and get another patient. She disappeared for about ten minutes, probably to the lounge or something. Then she returned into the room and declared, "There's no patients upstairs." I took a stroll upstairs and saw an amazingly large number of patients waiting to be seen. That was it. I blasted her, saying something like

"You're pissing me off." After an extended tirade, she promised to mend her ways. For the next few days, her actions improved, but then slid right back down again. That's when we transferred her off to some other duty assignment somewhere in the building. I never did see much of her again.

I was assigned another technician, DN Linda Pearson, who proved to be very capable and totally enjoyable to work with. She caught on quickly, was dependable, and was eager to work. And the best part of all was that she had the brightest smile around.

Periodically I helped out in the Acute Care Department, where I usually worked with another dentist and two technicians diagnosing and treating dental emergencies involving active duty personnel, spouses, children, and retirees. We saw irreversible pulpitis, periodontal abscesses, cracked teeth, broken teeth with sharp edges, pericoronitis, osteitis, soft tissue lacerations, subluxations, alveolar fractures, lateral luxations, avulsions, extrusions, and intrusions. We performed extractions and pulpectomies, placed temporary fillings, smoothed sharp edges of broken teeth, packed iodoform gauze and eugenol into dry sockets, and repositioned and splinted displaced teeth. We created incisions for obtaining drainage of acute abscesses, prescribed antibiotics and pain medications, did subgingival curettage and irrigation, recemented crowns, and reassured patients. After treating them, we referred them for definitive treatment to the appropriate department or, in the case of civilians, to a civilian dentist.

While working in Acute Care, LCDR George Hull, another University of Pittsburgh graduate, showed me how to use elevators to extract teeth. These instruments look something like a screwdriver and have multiple indications for use, among these to loosen teeth prior to the application of extraction forceps. I learned much more from him about this essential instrument than I did in the dental school curriculum, although I do remember taking the elevator from the basement to the second or third floors of the school often.

We used the SOAP format when we wrote in the patient charts:

S for "subjective data" (patient's symptoms or reason for visiting the clinic);

O for "objective data" (clinical observations, measurements, and test results);

A for "assessment" (the diagnosis); and

P for "plan" (treatment required to correct the problem).

The Acute Care Department was a great place to refine your diagnostic and emergency care skills. It was nice to be able to shift over to work here from time to time, and then return back to Operative again. This allowed for a bit more variety.

During the first week after my arrival at the naval base, I obtained a map and began exploring the wide expanse of Norfolk and Virginia Beach. Upon reaching the Atlantic oceanfront in Virginia Beach for the first time, the adrenalin flowed and my heart raced while I parked the car along the boardwalk. It was past dusk. I hopped out of the vehicle and rushed to lean against a metal railing that paralleled the beach. I couldn't believe it. Here I finally was—positioned to live at the ocean. The waves were crashing loudly onto the sand, looking intimidating and more powerful in the darkness. The wave crests seemed to glow in a whitish froth as stray lights from the streetlamps and hotels reflected onto the turbulence of the seawater.

I returned to the car and drove up Atlantic Boulevard, stopping at a McDonald's for dinner. It was then that I decided to find an apartment to rent somewhere around here. Back at the dental clinic, the word was that the Pembroke or Kempsville areas were the places to live, but I could not relate; those places were just too far away from the beach. Why join a navy, I thought, if you were going to live inland?

Within a few days I found an apartment at Chesapeake Beach, a short walk from the bay. The central location was an asset: I felt like I had my own quiet, personal beach close enough to work yet sufficiently near the ocean in the other direction. Now I was truly "on vacation," as I would routinely classify my situation to be.

When I was a kid growing up in Pennsylvania, I often heard people speak of a place where they vacationed that was called "Virginia Beach." I had never gone there, however. When I was assigned to my first duty station in Norfolk, I looked at a map and saw Virginia Beach right next to Norfolk. Now I was going there and it was then that I began to consider myself to be on vacation. Well, it was a working vacation anyway.

The commute to the naval base took about thirty to forty-five minutes, depending on the traffic flow, and reminded me of the bleak terrain in the *Road Warrior* movie. Almost every day there would be disabled vehicles stranded on the roadside, a white cloth wedged between the driver-side window and door frame, apparently some kind of distress signal. There were incessant fender-bender accidents or, at times, more severe wrecks. With so many people heading to such a big naval base each morning, it could be a real nightmare at times. You had to be on top of things at all moments, and a somewhat aggressive driver in order to keep up with the massive movement of automobiles.

After surviving each commute home from work, I spent as much time as possible at the beach. I got to know the various ocean smells. Most of the time there was a sweet scent which was my favorite, but at other times it was too fishy. I enjoyed jogging on the sand along the water's edge, dodging the approaching waves as they crawled higher up the beach.

When at last the warmer weather arrived, it was time to work on the tan. As one of the other lieutenants said, "Be sure to get a dark tan—it'll look good especially when we start wearing the summer white uniforms."

I bicycled around, exploring the uniquely different neighborhoods and tourist areas along the ocean. The dirt paths of Seashore State Park, a protected area of nearly three-thousand acres at the junction of the Chesapeake Bay and Atlantic Ocean, were a favorite destination.

I played on the clinic's softball team in a league that incorporated several different commands from the naval base and surrounding area. Games were held on the base near the water's edge, with views of the anchored aircraft carriers serving as a stunning backdrop while helicopters hovered above and other military aircraft flew overhead while we played ball. With sailors running to and fro down at the deepwater piers, there was no shortage of action and noise surrounding us as we competed on the softball field.

There was much to do in the Tidewater area. Nightclubs for the locals and tourists abounded. Oceana Naval Base had the legendary Officer's Club where women came from far and wide. This was where the Navy pilots hung out, often wearing their "pickle suits"—the olive green outfit worn while flying combat aircraft. You could have a beer inside one of several lounges or outside on the Flight Deck, a spacious dance floor and bar with great music.

On Fridays after work, I often went to TGIF at Waterside in Norfolk with my girlfriend to meet up with friends. The place was crowded with people, including many who arrived on boats, which would be moored to the docks and long piers along the water's edge. Usually there was a live band entertaining the masses. There were plenty of places for sit-down dining, but also a wide variety of street vendors from which to choose something to eat. In addition, there was a variety of unique shops through which to browse. It was a huge party.

The O Club at the Army's Fort Story was the place to be on Sunday evenings, starting at 7:00. Here you were partying on the sandy beach. Usually some individuals would dance atop the picnic tables. There were so many people gathering here that you had to park your car far away and catch a ride on a bus ferrying revelers back and forth.

There was an assortment of places where you could eat. At the Breezy Point Officer's Club was a fabulous seafood buffet on Friday evenings. Alaskan crab legs, shrimp scampi, seafood Newburg, baked potatoes, and steamed mussels were just a smidgeon of the food that was presented. On Sunday mornings, the Little Creek O Club had a great breakfast buffet. There was Tracy's, where you could have all the steamed shrimp you could eat. In addition, there were plenty of other fine establishments from which to pick, such as Alexander's on the Bay or the Raw Bar.

With Yorktown, Jamestown, and colonial Williamsburg nearby, the area was steeped in history. I lived very close to the place where the Jamestown colonists initially came ashore after their voyage across the Atlantic before heading further up the bay to establish the first permanent English settlement in the New World.

When you worked in such a large facility as the Naval Base clinic, you were destined to meet all kinds of colorful individuals. There was one commander who used to jog during lunchtime in big black combat boots. He looked like he was in great shape, so maybe the heavy-duty footwear contributed to this. There was a tall lieutenant who worked in the room near mine who used to loudly berate his patients if they presented with poor oral hygiene. His tone was demeaning and audible all the way down the passageway. "Do you know what this is?" he would scream with a southern drawl as he waved a toothbrush in the face of some intimidated patient.

During the course of each day, you would hear a diversity of stories told by coworkers who were from different parts of the United States, some being from foreign countries. The Big House resembled a giant locker room at times. Rumors circulated. "This one sleeps with this one; that one bought a new home on the lake . . ." And so on.

Someone brought in a comic strip, a most perceptive and humorous National Lampoon parody that featured a Navy Dental Corps stud prancing around in brown leather flight jacket, women swooning over him, as he takes charge. In another scene, there was a battlefield strewn with dead and critically wounded soldiers, one of them raising his hand, moaning and calling aloud, "Dentist! I need a dentist!" I thought, *a little humor like this could help rein in some of the overinflated egos that you find from time to time out there. Good for keeping things in perspective.*

In the summer months, we looked forward to the cookouts on Wednesday for lunch. You could have a burger, hot dog, or sausage sandwich. Several dental technicians cooked for the whole building's staff, doing a fabulous job with the logistics.

One time I handled a telephone call in the admin office from some Captain Jones. My task was just to take a simple message to be relayed to one of the administrative clerks. In the course of our phonecon I guess I forgot to say "sir" when addressing him, so he proceeded to chew me out. When I got off the phone, I said to myself, *better use that word more often from now on.*

Collateral duties were jobs we held in addition to the primary task of performing dentistry. I began working with the Sponsor Program Coordinator. I was to find sponsors for incoming personnel at the clinic. I looked for similarities in things such as rank and rate, marital status, and years of active military service in order to make a match. Then I would ensure that the chosen sponsor sent a letter of introduction and *Welcome Aboard Package* to the new member. I would assist sponsors when necessary. When the new member arrived, I would be one of the first to greet him or her. I dealt with officers and enlisted. I also required the new arrivals to fill out evaluation forms so we could monitor how we did. I met many people through this program.

Every six months we had to pass a *physical readiness test* (PRT) that involved stretching, pushups, sit-ups, and a one and a half mile run. You had two minutes to do as many sit-ups as you could, and two minutes for the pushups as well. The run had a maximum time limit that you needed to stay under. Standards required that each person's waist and neck diameters produce an acceptable body fat measurement. If you failed anything, you would have to set up a remedial training schedule so you could then attempt to pass a retest. The individual with the collateral duty of being in charge of the PRT had his hands full because, you could imagine, he might sometimes have to measure some fat old captain who might look him sternly in the eye and proclaim, sucking in his gut, "This better pass! Understand?" Usually the PRT Coordinator would then proceed to pull a little tighter on the measuring tape to arrive at a smaller number.

A *Hail-Farewell* party was held at the Navy Officer's Beach on 67th Street. This was a Navy event in which coworkers said goodbye to people leaving for their next duty station, while welcoming new arrivals to the command. For the departing personnel, it was an opportunity to acknowledge their accomplishments while stationed at the command. The Officer's Beach was a great place to have any event such as this. This beach was located farther north up the shore from the tourist-filled areas around 13th Street to the south.

Another naval tradition was the *Dining-In*, which was a formal Navy dinner also known as Mess Night. This event was a tradition which linked the present Navy to the founding of the nation and other naval history. The customs and traditions were observed to respect and honor the past while uniting the members of the mess in a "spirit of good fellowship and unity." Its origins could be traced back to the days of the Roman Empire when the Legionnaires held great banquets to celebrate their past triumphs and conquests. Later, Viking clans, on the occasion of their return from successful raids and forays against distant shores, held feasts and celebrations where great quantities of food and drink were served. Warriors who had conducted themselves with valor or distinction were honored. Mess Night could also be traced to the officers' messes of the Royal Navy, the Royal Marines, and the British Army.

At a Dining-In, a strict protocol was observed. For instance, there was a President of the Mess, a Vice President of the Mess, and a Guest of Honor. No one was permitted to leave the dining area without the permission of the President. The President rapped three times for attention and announced, "Gentlemen and Ladies, the grace." After the grace, the President seated the Mess with one rap of the gavel. After opening remarks by the President, the beef was paraded in to the tune of "Roast Beef of Olde England." A portion was offered to the Vice, upon which occasion he would determine whether or not the beef was fit for consumption. The President then announced the results of this determination. Dinner was served.

After dinner, formal toasting began. Toasting wine was passed from right to left in a clockwise fashion. As the bottles were emptied, the member having the empty bottle would raise it to indicate that a replacement was needed. The bottle was not to rest upon the table until the last glass was charged. Toasting glasses needed to be charged and at least raised to the lips; not to do so would be an insult to those being toasted.

When all glasses were charged, formal toasting began when the President rose and called for a toast "to the Commander-in-Chief." At the sound of the gavel, the Vice President seconded this by rising and addressing the Mess, "Gentlemen, Ladies, the Commander-in-Chief of the United States." Each member then stood and repeated in unison the toast, sipped the drink, and remained standing as the band played *Hail to the Chief.*

At the conclusion of the music, members and guests were again seated. Immediately after the first toast had been rendered, the President called for the "smoking lamp" to be lighted. Now and only now would smoking be permitted.

The President then initiated the remainder of the formal toasts, which included "Her Majesty the Queen of the United Kingdom," "The Congress of the United States," "Our Missing Comrades," "The Chief of Naval Operations," "The United States Marine Corps," "The Dental Corps," and "the United States Navy." Informal toasts came later, of which "inspired wit and subtle sarcasm" were much appreciated.

At the end of the toasting, the President rapped thrice with the gavel, at which time he asked the Vice to read the list of offenders who had violated the customs and traditions of this occasion. Suitable punishments were then declared. Violations included untimely arrival at the proceedings, smoking at the table prior to the lighting of the smoking lamp, loud and obtrusive remarks, foul language, improper toasting procedure, carrying cocktails into the dining room, wearing a clip-on bow tie at an obvious list, being caught with an uncharged glass, and leaving the dining area without permission from the President.

To end the night's formal activities, *Anchor's Away* was played, after which the President invited the Mess to join him at the bar for comradeship. The Dining-In was a wonderful example of one of the many rich traditions you could experience when you were a part of the Navy.

Back at the Naval Dental Center, opportunities for unique assignments arose. For example, on one occasion, volunteers were requested to go to sea for a week aboard a destroyer, one of the smaller

Navy ships that were fast in the water and had either air defense or antisubmarine functions. These sleek vessels were nicknamed "tin cans" and some were over five-hundred feet long. It seemed that this particular vessel's crew had slipped behind the acceptable dental readiness levels and so was badly in need of a boost. Mobile dental units were brought aboard along with one dentist and one technician.

Another opportunity for a unique assignment was the UNITAS Cruise, which would visit parts of Africa and then head down to South America, including a stay in Rio de Janeiro. The dentist who was selected to go came down with some exotic disease while in Africa, becoming pretty sick, and so another dentist from the Big House was to replace him. This replacement dentist packed his gear and made personal arrangements at home, but then about two days before he was to leave to rendezvous with the UNITAS Cruise, his orders were cancelled for some unknown reason. And that was it, just like that. This reinforced the saying, "Be flexible, young lieutenant." You had to learn to go with the flow, with the needs of the Navy, which could change often.

We had *duty* about once a month. Duty involved one doctor working all day treating emergencies, sleeping overnight at the clinic, ready to be awakened if an emergency patient presented. Typically, you could see about twenty patients on a Saturday or Sunday, and usually would have to be awakened from sleep at least once during the night by the on-duty dental technician. There was a specified duty room set up in which the duty doctor would sleep. After being aroused and rubbing your eyes to try to think clearly again, you would find a hurting and distressed man or woman sitting or pacing in the waiting room with an acute toothache awaiting desperately for some degree of relief as soon as could be possible.

Opportunities for continuing education abounded. Each week, one hour of our schedules was blocked off so we could attend a lecture presented by dentists from our clinic who were asked to present scientific papers or speak about some area of expertise. Often, one of the Advanced Clinical Program (ACP) fellowship students gave the talk. These senior dentists were in residence in a rigorous one-year course involving extensive didactic material and patient care. Topics presented at the weekly get-togethers included "Radiographic Interpretation," "Dental Photography," "Idiopathic Root Resorption," and "Mercury Hazard in Dental Amalgam," subjects only a dental person could love. Table clinics were sometimes scheduled during these Officer Training Meetings.

Periodically, there were *in-house courses* that lasted an entire day, worth seven hours of continuing education credit. Invitations to attend were forwarded to Navy dentists all over the world. There was, for example, an excellent course taught by Commander Henry St. Germain, an expert on operative dentistry and dental materials. Another outstanding course was on oral surgery, taught by LCDR John Kirby, who gave us all kinds of practical tips for dealing with infections and bone fractures, and on the mechanics of extracting teeth. Another time, there was a hands-on suturing course where we practiced various suturing techniques on slabs of meat. Only one week later after completing this program, I found occasion to utilize the newly-learned skills when some Marine required his lip to be sewn up following a traumatic incident. This in-house continuing education was more meaningful than CEU's received from some passing-through practitioner for the simple reason that it was more relevant. Presented by doctors who worked in the same building, more practical information was passed out, knowledge which helped everyone do a better and more efficient job handling cases and minimizing mistakes. Since everyone had a stake in things running smoothly, the courses tended to be more accessible and pragmatic.

The Navy also knew the value of having outside authorities lecture as well, serving to broaden the scope of what we could learn, and so outsiders such as civilians, Navy dentists assigned elsewhere, and dentists from other military branches also taught classes at the Big House from time to time.

Correspondence courses were offered through the mail so that even when you were assigned overseas or aboard ship, lacking access to shore-based continuing education, you could at least engage in self-study. While stationed at the Naval Base Norfolk, I completed correspondence courses in Combat Casualty and Endodontics. Textbooks and study materials were sent to participants, and you filled out a test upon completion of the required reading material. In addition, some shorter courses were available on videotape which could be mailed anywhere in the world.

Sometimes we could obtain orders to travel somewhere out of the local area to attend courses. During my years on active duty I was usually sent at least annually to the prestigious Naval Dental School in Bethesda, Maryland, where the Navy produced its specialists via a rigorous post-graduate education program. It was here that United States presidents traditionally received dental care. One time I had the opportunity to meet President George H.W. Bush's dentist there.

A Casualty Treatment Training Course (CTTC) was held and attended by me for five days in Norfolk in August of 1987. I'll explain a bit more about this since it went beyond our dental training to prepare us for wartime mass casualty situations we might find ourselves in while serving aboard ship or with the Marine Corps (Navy dentists were responsible for taking care of the Marines).

In a battlefield situation, the first thing to do was *triage*—the classification of casualties into priorities for treatment and evacuation. The goal of triage was to accomplish the greatest good for the greatest number, given the less-than-ideal battlefield conditions for performing medical treatment.

There were four triage categories: *Minimal*—ambulatory patients whose injuries were not disabling and did not require time-consuming treatment; *Immediate*—patients in immediate danger of death from asphyxia, hemorrhage, or shock, requiring swift treatment; *Delayed*—patients with grave injuries, such as chest wounds without respiratory failure, that did not present the same urgency for immediate treatment as in the immediate group; *Expectant*—hopelessly wounded patients requiring only alleviation of immediate stress.

Triage involved an *initial assessment* to determine the extent and nature of injuries on each casualty, and was divided into two surveys—a primary and a secondary. The *primary survey* involved rapid identification and treatment of life-threatening injuries. The *secondary survey* was a thorough head-to-toe evaluation which required more time and could be accomplished after all casualties had been primarily assessed and stabilized.

The primary survey involved the ABC's of life-saving. "A" was for **airway**—after determining why a patient's airway was closed, treatment could involve chin-lift, oral sweeps, suction, Heimlich maneuver, forceps retrieval, insertion airways, or crichothyroidotomy (needle or surgical). During any procedure to open an airway, we were careful not to aggravate any possible cervical spine (C-spine) fractures, which were expected with any trauma above the clavicle, and the only way to definitively rule out fracture was by taking a lateral C-spine radiograph or a Swimmer's View x-ray. Excessive movement of an injured C-spine could convert a fracture into neurological injury or partial or total loss of respiratory function.

"B" represented **breathing**. We needed to determine if a casualty was breathing and, if not, the reason why. Was breathing compromised because of a chest wound such as a sucking chest wound, tension pneumothorax, or flail chest? Or was respiration depressed for some other reason? Treatment involved chest tube placement, entubation, or artificial respiration.

"C" was for **circulation** (and hemorrhage control). Treatment included pulse monitoring, direct pressure, tourniquet, and pneumatic splinting. If cardiac tamponade was involved—a very serious condition in which central venous pressure was elevated while arterial pressure decreased and heart sounds were muffled—a procedure called pericardiocentesis would have to be performed.

"D" stood for **disability** and involved a brief neurological exam to establish the patient's level of consciousness. A simple AVPU test could be given: Was the patient alert? Did he respond to vocal or painful stimuli? Was the patient unresponsive?

"E" was for **expose**. This involved removal of clothing so a more thorough secondary survey could be begun.

During the secondary survey, the entire body was palpated and looked at. Any deviations from normal were noted. Radiographs, lab tests, and other diagnostic tests such as peritoneal lavage could be performed during this survey. Evidence of injuries, such as Ring Sign, Battle's Sign (ecchymosis in the mastoid region), hemotympanum (blood behind the tympanic membrane), and Opposum Sign (periorbital ecchymosis indicative of cribiform plate fracture) was documented.

Arriving at specific diagnoses of abdominal injuries was not as important as the fact that an abdominal injury existed and might need surgical intervention as soon as possible. If viscera were exposed outside of the abdominal cavity, a wet dressing needed to be placed over it.

Throughout the entire initial assessment, the following steps were to be accomplished whenever possible: administration of oxygen; treatment for shock; hook-up of two large-bore IV's; ECG monitoring; the establishment of a urinary catheter if not contraindicated by a high prostate; and insertion of a nasogastric tube if not contraindicated by conditions such as midface fracture or basilar fracture.

Constant reevaluation of each patient was required since a combat casualty's condition would be in a constant state of flux. And once initial assessment was concluded and conditions permitted, definitive care, such as major surgery, could be rendered.

The CTTC was exceptionally well done. Participants used models to simulate tracheal intubation and to practice inserting oropharyngeal, nasopharyngeal, and esophageal obturator airways. We also performed needle and surgical cricothyroidotomies, and then oxygenation with bag masks. We practiced bandaging and splinting, suturing, and wiring to immobilize fractured jaws. IV's and intramuscular injection techniques were practiced. Experience reading C-spine radiographs was gained. Each participant was given about twenty-five casualties to triage and treat. Urinary catheters and nasogastric tubes were inserted on models. We applied tourniquets, and practiced techniques for the debridement of soft tissues. Treatment for patients exposed to chemical, biological, and radiological agents was discussed, as well as treatment for hot and cold injuries. Treatment of burns was discussed at length, participants learning to identify burn types and estimate burn extent via the Rule of Nines. We learned how to relieve the pinching off of distal circulation to a burned limb by implementing escharotomy, which was the incision of the eschar to decrease edema pressure. We learned how to determine the amount of IV fluid and electrolytes needed in different burn situations.

And finally, after viewing films on the steps involved with the setup of a field hospital, and a filmed interview with LT Ware entitled, *The Beirut Experience*, about the role of dental personnel in the 1983 Marine Barracks bombing, the class was moved outdoors where teams had to proceed into the woods and find and treat casualties. They then had to transport them to safety by using appropriate litter carries while maneuvering through an obstacle course complete with psychological combat shock victims who impeded the rescue progress. The class was then bussed to another site to practice shipboard damage control.

In addition to CTTC, combat casualty medicine was also taught at the C-4 Course held somewhere in the Texas wilderness. After a few days of intense didactic study and lab exercises, including an actual demonstration of bullet penetration into live tissue (I think a goat was shot for this purpose), the group of medical personnel, who were from all branches of the military, was transported for several days of war games and camping in the outdoors, where triage and combat medicine was practiced.

A two-day course in Forensic Odontology was another exceptional continuing education event featured at the Naval Dental Center. It involved the identification of deceased individuals through dental examination and review of previous dental records. Participants were placed into a mock mass disaster scenario. Actual human remains were used as well as an assortment of radiographs and dental charts.

We organized ourselves into groups according to task. The antemortem dental records team had to determine who was involved in the disaster, locate and procure dental records from a variety of sources throughout the United States, arrange for the delivery of those materials to the disaster identification center, and develop composite antemortem records for each victim using the supplied evidence. This task was made more complex because dentists use different, nonstandardized charting techniques throughout the United States and the rest of the world. In addition, some records were not clear or complete. And of course some records could not be obtained.

The postmortem dental examination team performed exams on whatever human remains were retrieved following the disaster. Facial dissection often was necessary. Full mouth radiographs were essential. Data was charted.

The third job of forensic odontology could now be accomplished: look for positive identification matches between antemortem and postmortem dental records. This was a challenge because of all the limitations that presented.

In July of 1987, after working in the Operative Department for about four months, I moved to the Oral Hygiene Department, where I would manage about five to eight dental technicians who performed prophies (*dental prophylaxis*; the scaling and polishing of teeth). This was an opportunity to exercise leadership and management skills. I reviewed instrument sharpening techniques and scaling procedures with the technicians. I evaluated their job performances and managed any glitches that might arise each day. I learned a lot from them; for example, from one tech I discovered that a 5-T carver worked quite well in removing calculus (tartar) from the broad lingual surfaces of mandibular anteriors.

After about a month of working in Oral Hygiene, I was selected to work in the Endodontics Department upstairs. The first day there, the Department Head, CDR Jeff Hutter, took me aside and, using a small blackboard, presented the best lecture on endodontic diagnosis and treatment I had ever had. There were many great lectures in dental school, but this one was a step above. CDR Hutter was an individual filled with unlimited energy. Sometimes he would have three patients going at once and, after finishing those, he would immediately emerge from the room and ask if there were any more patients needing to be seen. In later years, he was to become the president of the American Association of Endodontists and dean of Boston University's Goldman School of Dental Medicine.

All day long, we did root canal therapy. There were two Advanced Clinical Program students working in Endo. They frequently referred to the scientific research to support their diagnoses and treatment choices, often citing "Seltzer and Bender," for example. We used preprinted cardboard cards to record working lengths and other detailed data about each case that we worked on, and affixed all the radiographs to this card. It was a very nice way to capture each case for future reference. One day, one of the ACP students showed me a final radiograph of a maxillary molar case he had just completed and there was a very large amount of root canal sealer extruded outside of the tooth's apex. He looked at me, shrugging his shoulders, and declared, "Oh, my God, I obturated his brain!"

Other dentists working in the building often came in to ask questions about endodontics. By this time, I was feeling like a true team player, very much enjoying the opportunity to interact with the other providers and assist patients with tighter coordination of their treatment plans. I had become very familiar with how things worked in the clinic and so I felt helpful in keeping patient flow running as smoothly as possible, a task often difficult in such a large facility that was departmentalized.

Then during one of the clinic's softball games, I injured my right wrist while sliding into second base. When the pain failed to subside after about five days, I checked in to Medical and they discovered I had a broken wrist. A cast was placed, extending from my fingers to my elbow. A week later, I had a reevaluation with a different Navy physician who noted that I had the wrong type of cast. The one I had extended only to just before my elbow and so allowed me to bend my arm. He noted that it should have extended up to my shoulder. But since I had no significant pain and was functioning well, he decided it would be okay to stay with the shorter cast. This was fortunate for me because a longer cast would have knocked me out from doing endodontics; the shorter cast gave me a greater range of motion. To further increase my ability to remain working in Endo, I went to the dental lab just down the hall and had one of the lab techs use a large acrylic bur to grind away some of the plaster from between my thumb and forefinger. This gave me more use of the essential opposable thumb. I also had to deal with infection control issues so that the higher ranking officers didn't begin questioning the appropriateness of my continuing to work on patients in lieu of getting transferred to some desk job away from the action. I rigged up a plan: before seeing each patient, I wrapped the cast in plastic wrap, then secured it with rubber bands and tape. This raised a few eyebrows, but proved to be satisfactory.

With the broken wrist, the most difficult thing to do was give anesthesia, since I had to maneuver my body into contorted positions in order to line everything up right. It took every ounce of energy to concentrate on getting this right. To file canals, I had to focus, let's say, three times as much as usual. I soon learned to use my left hand as well as my right for instrumenting, a valuable skill that persisted into the future, greatly enhancing patient care.

One day, there was a dentist from a ship who came in for root canal therapy on a molar. He was scheduled with me. I offered to transfer him to a different dentist to have the treatment done since I had the cast on my arm and felt because he was a dentist he might feel I could not do the job fast enough. But he surprised me when he said he preferred that I did the treatment anyway. He just wanted to get it done as soon as possible and didn't want to have to reschedule the appointment. So I completed it successfully, and confidence grew. I told people jokingly that "I'm getting really denser obturations now because of the extra weight of the cast."

From the Commanding Officer came a directive for each department to update its Procedure Manual. This manual was a formal document that portrayed information about department policy which could be read by any provider rotating through that department so to orient and familiarize that person with the operations there. The collateral duty of updating the manual in Endo was assigned to me. I conducted informal interviews with the technicians and doctors and referenced existing documents. The techs said the previous manual was uninteresting, had many obsolete statements, and was "too difficult to read." There was too much unnecessary repetition and verbosity. I tried to improve upon these shortcomings, and in the rearranging tried to keep it general so to allow flexibility so as not to get bound down excessively to rigid rules that would suppress innovation. It was a great experience in administration and editing.

After serving three of the four months of the endo rotation, the Branch Director told me, "We have an emergency and need to send someone who can do dentistry over to the shipyard across the river." They had some problem with staffing and needed a replacement ASAP. So I moved to the Norfolk Naval Shipyard (NNSY) in Portsmouth, Virginia for the next eight months.

NNSY had a small dental clinic that employed three general dentists and one prosthodontist. This would be a great place to practice a wider range of dentistry than was possible in the large departmentalized Big House. At the Naval Base clinic, if a patient needed periodontal treatment, he or she was sent to the Periodontal Department. If she needed a crown, she would be sent to the Prosthodontic Department. If the patient required a tooth extraction, he would have to go to the Oral Surgery Department. Root canal? Go to the Endodontics Department. Everything was departmentalized with a specialized division of labor.

In contrast, at NNSY you could be more of a general dentist. For example, I did exams and treatment planning, operative, emergencies, endodontics, periodontics, and some prosthodontics. There was also a dental lab with which I could interact.

I started doing periodontal exams with patients who needed it. I informed them of the diagnosis of periodontal disease, the etiology, sequelae, and treatment. Using a typodont and other visual aids, I demonstrated pockets and flossing technique. When they later proved themselves to be motivated and showed signs of improved oral hygiene, we proceeded to scaling and root planing, followed by a one-month reevaluation.

Navigating around inside a shipyard could be a challenging task because of all the clutter. There were railroad tracks spreading out in various directions, people walking and running about, and a wide assortment of obstacles of varying shapes and sizes strewn about. There was a lot of loud noise, like that from jackhammers and big trucks and machines. There was dust in the air. In fact, one day I got something in my eye as I walked around outside the clinic. Fortunately the Medical Clinic was in our same building. A Warrant Officer was able to remove some kind of foreign object from the surface of my eye.

It was impressive to see what a ship in drydock looked like, with its huge underbelly exposed, outside of the water. While I worked at the shipyard, there was one ship in drydock. The whole vessel was hoisted in the air so that the hull could be repaired or refurbished. Sometimes during lunch we would jog by it and then around all the obstacles inside the rest of the yard, and along the Elizabeth River, where there were some scenic views to take in. And of course there were always seagulls flying around.

One morning I went to the shipyard's daycare center with LCDR Roger Houk to teach the preschoolers about oral hygiene. He came up with a great idea to get four little volunteers to slip white pillowcases over their heads and then push their heads through a small slit that was cut into the material so that their heads poked through. They were to pretend they were teeth. We had them stand in a row next to each other just like in the dental arch. Then we demonstrated how to brush, using a giant toothbrush on their fronts and backs and on the top of their heads. And for flossing, we used a thick rope, manipulating it with proper flossing technique in between the children. Everybody had fun. In fact, we probably had to allow a second, and maybe a third, group of four enthusiastic kids to dress up as teeth before it was all over.

LCDR Houk never used topical anesthetic prior to giving dental injections because, as he said, it really did not do anything that was significantly beneficial, except perhaps have a placebo effect for some very nervous patients. The real secret to relatively painless injections was in your demeanor and actual technique. I adopted this strategy with the exception that I would use it only whenever a patient specifically requested it. I found this to be very successful.

A word about third molars (*wisdom teeth*), which often caused problems. If they erupted into the mouth into positions that made it difficult for individuals to accomplish effective daily plaque removal, then caries and periodontal disease could result. Sometimes, owing to their malposition, they would be partially covered by a flap of soft tissue under which food and plaque accumulated, resulting in pericoronitis where the soft tissue became inflamed or abscessed, necessitating emergency treatment.

The standard policy toward third molars was to remove them if they were likely to cause a problem. The easiest time to remove them was between the ages of sixteen and twenty-two. Each year beyond that, extraction became increasingly more difficult because the roots locked in, the bone became denser, there was greater chance for complications, and healing was not as efficient. If a patient was going to be deployed somewhere where access to care would be limited, such as on a submarine or in some remote duty station, removal of these teeth was given a higher priority. For example, because of the nature of their specific mission, the location of submarines had to be kept top secret. If a submariner developed a problem with his third molars while on a secret deployment and the corpsman aboard could not handle it entirely, the boat might have to surface in order to transfer the individual so he could get the proper care, thus drawing attention to its no-longer-secret whereabouts.

In the Navy, orthodontic treatment (braces) was available on a very limited basis. The Navy orthodontists would treat active duty members if there was a malocclusion present that either threatened the longevity of the dentition or prevented adequate function. Most of the cases they could treat required orthognathic surgery. Orthodontic treatment was contraindicated in cases such as where esthetics alone was involved or in crowding cases where reasonable oral hygiene could adequately protect the dentition and surrounding tissues.

We routinely recommended that servicemembers not seek treatment from a civilian orthodontist unless they had sufficient tour length in a nondeployable unit to complete the treatment. Otherwise, they might end up wasting a lot of money on treatment begun but which could not be completed if they were to be summoned to deploy away from dental support.

At NNSY, I began noticing that military dentists experienced "geographic successes." At the Big House, patients got as a dentist whoever was next in line. That dentist would treat the patient, and then very often never see that patient again. The dentist was thus unable to follow up to evaluate how his treatment held up over time. At other duty stations, certainly there were occasions when you might indeed see a patient multiple times while you were assigned to a two or three-year duty station. But you might, for example, do a root canal filling, crown, or other restoration, and then observe no problems with it over the next year or two. Then the patient or you moved halfway across the world when duty stations changed. But then four years later a problem might develop with the tooth as a result of some unintentional inadequacy in your technique. You would never know about it, however, as would civilian dentists who usually were able to follow up treatment on their own patients for years and thus learn from the experience.

I began witnessing an amazing diversity throughout the Navy Dental Corps with the way T2 exams were documented in patient charts. Depending on where you worked, different commands devised very different formats. Many were verbose to the extreme. Others were muddled with complexity, made more complicated than necessary. A few were short and concise. Some places designed their own pre-inked stampers to rapidly get a printed format onto the standard progress notes page, while others would use an entire preprinted page that would have to be enclosed inside the patient's chart. It was fascinating to observe the variety.

In fact, over the years in the Navy I saw a wide assortment of printed forms used by different dental officers, including oral surgery consent, oral surgery post-op instructions, and TMD evaluations. I collected copies of these as well as the T2 setups and was able to pick and choose the best of each and devise my own streamlined forms over the years. This was a nice advantage to working in a large organization such as the military.

Having worked at both a large and a small clinic certainly made for a great combination of invaluable instruction. Dental skills were sharpened and knowledge was gained. The experiences served as a perfect springboard to an operational tour of duty.

PART THREE

WELCOME ABOARD

In 1988 I received orders to report to the USS John F. Kennedy for a two-year operational tour. A letter from Captain Richards congratulated me on my selection to this assignment and stated, correctly, that a tour on an aircraft carrier would be exciting and certainly a high point of a dental career in the U.S. Navy.

To prepare for this duty station, I read *Supercarrier*, the essential book by George Wilson about life aboard this ship. I also attended the two-day fire-fighting school in Norfolk, where I remember entering a small building, guiding a heavy fire hose along with the rest of my team as we maneuvered between metal railings atop a narrow iron catwalk that looked down upon a rather large fire to our front and sides, nearly encircling us. I was immediately impressed by the great amount of heat that emanated from the flames. After we finally extinguished the conflagration and began to withdraw from the building, figuring we were finished with the drill, a reflash occurred, so we had to reenter and proceed deeper into the building to renew the fight. This time my arms got so hot I thought they were going to catch fire. The hands-on training evoked a sincere appreciation for the demands of shipboard firefighting.

I reported for duty aboard the ship in July of 1988. She was anchored at her homeport of Norfolk. After leaving my car in the vast parking lot, I looked up and was in awe of the great number of massive grey ships tied to the piers, lined up in a row along the waterfront. The odor of grease and oil mixed in with the familiar scents of the ocean created an unforgettable smell that pervaded the air around the piers. There was an abundance of human activity on both sides of the metal fence that separated the road adjacent to the parking lot from the piers as sailors wearing work dungarees and the black baseball caps emblazoned with their duty station name scurried about doing their jobs. Several small cranes and other vehicles darted to and fro. There were frequent announcements made over loudspeakers aboard the vessels, which could be heard even from where I parked the car. This was *the real Navy*.

I proceeded through the security gate and was inundated with salutes and "Good morning, Sir!" salutations as I strode the very long distance down the pier to the entrance to the ship. My arm must have been tired from so many salutes. I eventually reached the portable metal staircase that would convey me from the pier upward to the ship. I climbed the steps to the top, high above ground level.

At the top of the ladder (stairs) stood the Officer of the Deck (OOD). To board the ship, I followed the protocol dictated by naval tradition. First, I turned toward the ensign (the flag of the United States) and saluted it. Then I turned to the OOD and, while saluting him, stated, "Request permission to come aboard." He replied, "Permission granted," as he returned my salute. Then I entered the myriad of passageways inside the world's largest conventionally powered aircraft carrier.

The USS Kennedy had eight decks and eleven levels. Decks and levels were the equivalent of a building's floors or stories. The hangar deck and each floor below it were called *decks*; the floors above the hangar deck were denoted *levels*. The hangar deck was the place where aircraft could be stored, maintained, and repaired.

The ship, at 242 feet in height from keel to mast top, was taller than a seventeen-story building. The overall length was 1072 feet and, if stood on end, was taller than the Empire State Building. Her breadth at the flight deck level was 270 feet. She displaced 82,000 tons of water, and had two anchors, each weighing thirty tons.

The Kennedy was propelled by eight steam boilers and four five-bladed propellers, each twenty-one feet in diameter, and could travel at a speed greater than thirty knots, which was more than thirty-five-plus miles per hour, with a horsepower greater than two-hundred thousand.

About 5,222 people would live and work aboard this vessel on any one day during deployment with the aircraft. About 15,666 meals were served aboard ship daily.

The ship was named for the thirty-fifth president of the United States of America. Some said his spirit and dedication guided the crew in day-to-day operations, helping to produce the degree of success achieved and the fine worldwide reputation the ship had attained over the years. The keel was laid 22 Oct 64 at the Newport News Shipbuilding and Drydock Company in Virginia. President Kennedy's daughter, Caroline, christened the ship in May of 1967, during ceremonies held at Newport News, Virginia.

John F. Kennedy once explained that *it is the fate of this generation . . . to live with a struggle we did not start, in a world we did not make. But the pressures of life are not always distributed by choice. And while no nation has ever been faced by such a challenge, no nation has ever been so ready to seize the burden and glory of freedom.* He was well aware that to meet that challenge, strength was needed as a partner to idealism. Because he recognized that fact, he requested the funds from Congress in 1963 to build the mighty ship that would be named after him.

In September of 1970, USS Kennedy was ordered to the Mediterranean Sea in response to a crisis developing in the Middle East. She sailed again to the Mediterranean the following year, during which time the deployment was extended due to increased activity in the war in Southeast Asia.

In 1982, USS Kennedy won her eighth Battle "E" efficiency award and fourth Golden Anchor retention award. In 1983, the ship was called upon to support operations around Beirut, Lebanon, where the growing crisis there necessitated the ship remain on station into 1984. That year, the USS Kennedy received her ninth Battle "E," the Silver Anchor Award for retention, the RADM Flatley Award for safety, and the Battenburg Cup for being the overall "best ship in the Atlantic Fleet."

In July of 1986, USS Kennedy served as the centerpiece of a vast international naval armada during the International Naval Review in honor of the 100th Anniversary and Rededication of the Statue of Liberty. The ship hosted President and Mrs. Reagan for this event. It had gained a reputation as the showboat of the United States Navy.

The Captain of the USS Kennedy was Captain Hugh D. Wisely, a decorated fighter pilot from New Jersey who became the first Vietnam veteran credited with shooting down two enemy aircraft. He was also shot down by groundfire during a Hanoi strike and later rescued somewhere on the border of Laos and North Vietnam. In 1979 he took command of the Blue Angels. He had logged over 5450 flight hours, 800 carrier landings, and over 350 combat missions in Vietnam.

It was aboard this famous ship that I was fortunate to have been assigned. After checking in, there were only two weeks for me to get settled in before the ship and her crew would depart for a six-month deployment. The Dental Department's crew was exceedingly helpful in preparing me, advising me what to bring and what to generally expect. The Department Head, LCDR Steve Wallace, from Texas, urged me to spend a weekend aboard prior to the deployment while we were still in port so I could get more familiar with the environment. But I had a busy enough social life and wanted no part of losing a weekend ashore, especially since I would live aboard the ship for the next half of a year anyway, during which I figured I would have plenty of time to get familiar with the surroundings. So I did not take him up on his advice.

On Tuesday, August 2, 1988, the USS Kennedy departed Norfolk to cross the Atlantic Ocean and enter the Mediterranean Sea, not to return to the United States until February of 1989, more than six months later. She got underway along with seventeen other Atlantic Fleet ships. All together, the entire Kennedy Battle Group included more than 14,000 sailors and marines. During this deployment, ten different ports were visited, with eleven port calls, and there was to be one military confrontation.

I said goodbye to my girlfriend the night before departure. Early in the morning my neighbor dropped me off at the pier. As I walked toward the ship, lugging the last of my carry-on belongings, I was touched by all the sad goodbyes between sailors and their loved ones. For some there were tears, and for others who had already been through this many times there was either quiet reflection or awkward attempts at humor. Once aboard ship, most of the men were reticent and just went about their work as if to take their minds off the family separations. I was struck by the overall silence.

I helped *man the rails* as the anchors were lifted and the tugboats began to slowly tow the enormous ship away from the pier. This tradition was to have white-uniformed sailors standing at attention lined up all the way around the outer periphery of the empty flight deck. It must have been an impressive sight to anyone looking at the ship from afar. I stood there and took in the forlorn quietude as the ship was pulled down the bay.

At last the tugs broke free and the USS Kennedy began steaming by her own power. "The ship is underway!" was announced over the 1MC (intercom system). The rail-manning staff was dismissed. I made my way down the ladders to the Dental Department to discover there were no patients scheduled since the crew was busy with the priority of getting underway. I eventually went topside to the port sponson, which was a projection from the side of the ship from where excellent views of the water could be had. We had passed through the Chesapeake Bay Bridge-Tunnel and were miles offshore into the Atlantic Ocean. I was fascinated by the deep blue hue of the ocean. Before this, I had only witnessed the shallower blue-green waters near the shoreline and was never out this far away from land. It was a distinctly different color way out here, at this ocean depth.

Walking through the passageways of the ship, with the vast collection of pipes, wires, cables, and valves seeming to crawl up the light green and white bulkheads, made me wonder how safe this place was. I began to experience the various noises about the ship. And land legs had to adapt to being at sea as I began to feel the slight rocking of the deck. When walking down the passageways

I had to lift my feet high up over the knee-knockers every time leaving a compartment or else risk tripping over the raised metal barrier flange. I also frequently found myself getting lost.

I was issued black steel-toed boots, earplugs for hearing protection, a heavy green winter coat, and a white turtle-neck sweatshirt with "Dental Officer" stenciled on the back. During the first couple weeks at sea, I also took a Ship Familiarization course recommended to all new personnel to help them get oriented to the new environment.

I did *egress drills* in which I was blindfolded and had to make my way from the Dental Department up the ladder and outside onto the nearest *weather deck* (deck exposed to the outside). I also had to do this from my stateroom. The intent was to get shipmates used to what conditions would be like in the event of a loss of lighting or if we became blinded during a wartime situation and had to find a way out of the ship's interior spaces.

The first berthing I had was a six-man stateroom just below one of the ship's catapults, near the flight deck on the O-3 level. What a thunderous sound there was when aircraft launched and landed just above where I slept. I hardly ever ran into any roommates since we all had very different work hours around the clock. Someone was always asleep in the room and lights were generally out. The dental officers razzed me up since my stateroom was "in pilot country," way up on the O-3 level in the area where the pilots lived. In contrast, the staterooms of the dental officers were way down below on the third deck.

Occasionally during the cruise a civilian technical representative (tech rep) would come aboard for a few days or weeks and occupy the sixth berth. One of the tech reps looked like a mountain man with large beard and mustache, definitely standing out in appearance from the active duty personnel with their shortly-cropped hair and uniforms.

One day, I got talking to one of my roommates and mentioned I had read *Supercarrier* and he said, nonchalantly, "Oh yeah. I think I'm on page twenty-two." He was LCDR Doug Millar, the S-3A Viking pilot described in the book who was awarded a Medal of

Commendation for his efforts in stopping a runaway aircraft which had no brakes following its landing on the flight deck. He kept the aircraft moving in circles on the deck, striving to maintain control as the ship pitched and rolled. He tried not to roll over the side into the ocean or crash into a parked plane, possibly touching off an explosion. If he ejected, he might get slammed into the steel hull or land in the water too close to the carrier and get sucked into the propellers. He kept making tight turns as heroic flight deck personnel risked their own lives in several attempts to capture the aircraft's wheels with chocks and chains. Ultimately they were able to secure the plane.

Later in the deployment, LCDR Millar moved out of the six-man room into a two-man stateroom on the third deck, several "stories" down and deeper inside the ship's interior. He asked me if I wanted to move in with him, so I seized the opportunity. The new room would be more conveniently and centrally located for me.

We had not been out to sea for one day when "Man Overboard!" was called. All personnel immediately mustered at their work centers. Petty Officer Pat Pellet, in charge of mustering dental work center personnel, checked off the names of individuals appearing and, when everyone was accounted for, submitted the roster. Anyone not appearing for muster could be the person who had fallen overboard. We watched over the ship's TV as the rescue crew successfully located and pulled the hapless individual from the frigid water. He had been hurling garbage bags over the fantail, but forgot to let go of one of the bags. Into the water he went. Fortunately he was able to use the bag as a flotation device and was rescued quickly.

From the start of the cruise I posted a calendar on the bulkhead of my dental operatory and colored in each day's block with a blue pencil as the date passed. At the halfway point of three months, it looked good to see so many blue squares and to know we were *over the hump.*

LCDR Don Primley, the ship's oral surgeon, posted a large wall map of the world. Each day he plotted our course across the Atlantic and within the Med.

During the first week of the cruise, Chief Reulito Gonzalez, hailing from the Philippines, brought the dental crew newly-printed copies of the port schedule. Prior to this we could only guess as to where we would be going. Rumor had it that due to congressional budget cuts, we would be forced to cut down on the ship's steaming time to save money. The USS Kennedy was not a nuclear-powered vessel that could go without refueling for perhaps as long as fifteen years. Instead, she required relatively frequent *underway replenishment*. Some said it cost a million dollars a day to expend as much fuel as we used up. With these reported budget cutbacks came less steaming time on the open seas and more time in port, which was agreeable to the crew. Actually, I do not know how true all of that was; maybe it was just a morale booster.

Before coming to the ship, it was explained to me that the dental readiness of the crew had been slipping. They needed someone who could turn out fast, efficient dentistry, and hoped that I could help. I accepted the challenge; it became my own personal mission to "pound out amalgams," as one lieutenant back at the Naval Dental Center once put it, and do whatever else was necessary to get the ship's dental readiness up.

To accomplish that, I concentrated on tightly organizing my DOR and then reviewing with my assistant, DN Jeff Denter, exactly what I expected of him. DN Denter had built a reputation as an angry person with a short fuse. He wanted to leave the Navy. He did not want to be deployed away from his family. I gave him a clear set of directives and he responded extremely well. We got along very well, working efficiently and having fun in the process. The Department Head was elated—he had finally found a niche for DN Denter. In fact, Denter responded so favorably that he earned Sailor of the Quarter, an honor that no one ever thought he would get.

Sometime during the two weeks it took to cross the Atlantic Ocean, the aircraft of the air wing joined the ship, landing one by one on the flight deck, in the celebrated *fly-on*. The air squadrons that hooked up with us included Attack Squadron 75 and Fighter Squadrons 14 and 32 from Oceana Naval Air Station in Virginia Beach; Carrier Airborne Early Warning Squadron 126 from the

Norfolk Naval Air Station; Anti-submarine Squadron 22 from
Cecil Field, Florida; Helicopter Anti-submarine Squadron 7 from
Jacksonville, Florida; Marine Attack Squadron 533 from Cherry
Point, North Carolina; and Tactical Electronic Warfare Squadron
130 from Whidbey Island, Washington.

For now, I'll give you an idea of what a day at sea could be like.
I'll start with my stateroom on the third deck—keep in mind that
I actually would not live in that room until December during the
Med Cruise, after I moved down from the O-3 level way above. But
since I would live on the third deck for the majority of this tour of
duty, I'll discuss that room in the following account.

A typical day at sea began when my alarm clock awakened me
at 0600. If only there was a snooze button, there'd be times I would
have hit it and slept longer. Instead, my clock lacking this function,
I forced myself to sit up in bed so I would not fall back asleep
without having the benefit of another wakeup call.

I turned on the reading lamp above, my eyes slowly adjusting
to the newly-found light. The ceiling was not far from the top of
my head. Dangling my leg down from the side of the upper bunk
bed, I searched for the edge of the lower bunk. Finding it, I put
my weight upon it and jumped down onto the hard, polished deck
below. My roommate was already gone. I noticed a pile of papers
on my desk and remembered I had a minor administrative project
to finish that day.

The grunts and groans of the ship could be heard as it churned
through the water, metallic twisting and flexing environing me
incessantly where I dwelled, deep within the confines of the aircraft
carrier. George Wilson got it right when he wrote in Supercarrier,
"Our room was just above the waterline. Its long distance from the
flight deck muffled the sounds of the controlled crashes of carrier
landings five stories above us. But even a room this deep inside the
carrier was assaulted by the special noises of a live warship: the throbs
and squeaks of pumps, the whir of fans, the clanging of machinery,
the piercing whistles prefacing announcements over loudspeakers,
the banging of doors, and the high-pitched screams of jet engines."
Sounds like an uncomfortable environment, but it was easy for me

to get used to, especially since I had lived right in the heart of a bustling busy city for four years.

After a few morning stretches, I put on a robe and flip-flops, and grabbed a towel and soap. Leaving the stateroom, I shut the door behind me and walked not more than one-hundred feet down the maze-like passageway, making a couple of turns, to the head. As usual at this time, there were other people staggering half-asleep to get ready for the day.

It always struck me as fascinating that the toilet bowls were filled with saltwater. Just knowing this made the water in the bowl appear so different to me, despite the reality that it actually looked like any normal toilet water ashore. Maybe I expected some sea creature to be lurking there.

The shower stalls were like stainless steel cabinets that did not have much room inside. There seemed to be no symmetric plan guiding where each stall was located along the winding passageways. They were arranged haphazardly. There was an adequate number to accommodate the population of personnel living in this neighborhood of the third deck.

When I was young, my father spoke at times of *navy showers*: you would wet yourself, then shut off the water, then lather with soap, finally getting the water flowing again to rinse. This conserved water. A ship's crew had to constantly make freshwater from ocean water using an elaborate desalination process. In contrast to navy showers was a *Hollywood shower* in which you would just let the water discharge for a long time without any concern for restricting the volume. These kinds of showers were frowned upon since no one wanted to run out of fresh water.

One morning when in the shower, the water temperature changed suddenly for some unknown reason from lukewarm to scalding hot within seconds. I was forced back against the wall of the stall before I could shut off the faucet, so I got a mild burn to the chest. From that day forth I approached the showers with caution, always ready to bolt away from the water stream if necessary. It did happen again from time to time, but never as hot as that first occurrence.

The Navy uniform was worn at all times while aboard ship, except obviously of course at times such as when we were sleeping, working out, or going on liberty. I dressed into the working khaki uniform which was made of cotton as opposed to the polyester uniform typically worn at duty stations ashore. The more flammable polyester was prohibited here because the living and working conditions as existed aboard a warship were dangerous enough and you did not want to magnify your risks. The cotton was much safer—and more comfortable, too.

I left my laundry bag at the designated location for pickup. It was a mesh container that we filled with dirty laundry and then secured closed with a large pin. This entire package would be thrown into some giant washing machine and run through an agitated wash cycle. Our clothing was stenciled with the first letter of our last name followed by the last four digits of our social security number to allow for easier identification just in case anything escaped from the netting.

The smells of breakfast began emanating from the deck above. I climbed the silver ladder from "Officer's Country," where my stateroom was located, to the second deck. The ladder bounced and clanged as I ascended it. Breakfast was served just down the passageway from here.

As I mentioned earlier, the dining area for officers was called a *wardroom*, of which there were two on the ship. This one—the one located near my stateroom—was the main one, primarily used by the officers of *ship's company* (the personnel attached to the ship permanently, as opposed to the air wing officers who lived aboard only during certain deployments). The air wing officers primarily used the forward wardroom, which was found closer to the bow of the ship. Occasionally I dined there, for a change of pace and to be entertained by conversations with the lively pilots.

For breakfast, I served myself cold cereal, toast, and a glass of orange juice. Sometimes I would get in the usually short line in front of the kitchen and order scrambled eggs or French toast.

I picked up a copy of the ship's daily newspaper, *The Bird Farm News*, and perused it while I ate. There were a few other officers quietly eating breakfast around me, and we engaged in periodic conversation.

By 0645, I finished breakfast and headed to the Dental Department, located just down the passageway. As you can see, everything was centrally located. It was so much more convenient than having to wake up much earlier as I did when the ship was anchored in Norfolk and I lived off base and had to be able to make the commute to work on time over the busy highways. In contrast, this was real living.

I descended the ladder into the Kennedy's Dental Department. Already there were two shipmates sitting atop storage boxes topped off with padded cushions in the small, compressed waiting room, in anticipation of sick call at 0700. Whenever the ship was at sea, we held sick call for an hour beginning at this time, and again at 1800 in the evening. This was intended to be a time when people experiencing dental problems could walk in without an appointment for treatment of the problem. Of course, emergencies could occur at any time; for example, midway through the day some boiler technician might whap his jaw against an unexpectedly protruding pipe, with a resulting fractured tooth and lacerated lip. In that circumstance, he could check in to the dental clinic at any time.

Legend had it that during the ship's construction and issuance of 2,400 miles of design blueprints, the engineers forgot to include a place for dentistry. Someone eventually brought the oversight to their attention, and they decided to rip down some stateroom bulkheads to create the dental spaces. The result was that the Kennedy's Dental Department was smaller than the other carriers'. Nevertheless, despite the narrow passageways and reduced area, the spaces reserved to serve as a dental clinic afloat were more than suitable for getting the job done.

Dental services provided by the clinic included operative dentistry, endodontics, prosthodontics, periodontics, extractions, intravenous conscious sedation, general anesthesia, biopsies, repair of traumatic wounds to the head and neck, scaling and polishing of teeth, emergency care, and routine examination and treatment planning. All services were provided free of charge.

The dental staff consisted of one oral surgeon, three general dentists, and eight to twelve enlisted support personnel. The mission of the ship's Dental Department was to provide services that helped prevent or correct disabilities which could hinder military personnel from carrying out their duties in support of the overall mission of the Armed Services of the United States.

There were six dental operatories. An *operatory* included a stool for the dentist and one for the assistant, the air and water unit, the suction apparatus, overhead light, and that comfortable chair that patients frequently say they would love to have in their living room back home. With regard to that patient chair, the dental technicians who were on call after-hours would often throw a blanket over themselves and sleep in the chair since they had to remain in Dental all night.

The deck in Dental was painted a glossy mud-brown color, while the bulkheads were generic white. A silver *scuttlebutt* (drinking fountain) was affixed to the waiting room bulkhead. When you climbed down the ladder to enter the dental department, if you then turned left and proceeded all the way to the end of the narrow main passageway, you would enter the x-ray room, which was complete with a panoramic x-ray machine, dark room, and conventional x-ray machine. The panoramic ("pano") x-ray machine was the large device that nearly surrounded the patient as he bit on a soft mouthpiece while the x-ray nosecone moved around his head. The result was the five-inch by twelve-inch rectangular image that showed the patient's jaw, sinuses, and teeth. Among other things, this type of x-ray was particularly good for visualizing the location of third molars which were not captured in full on other x-rays. A doctor could use this film to evaluate potential risks if the third molars were to be extracted.

The conventional x-ray machine was used to take *bitewings* and *periapical* x-rays. Bitewings were the pair of routine x-rays taken, one on each side of the face, as the patient bit his teeth together. These views were primarily used to detect caries in between the teeth, which could not be seen directly in the mouth. The periapical radiograph allowed the doctor to see the root apices of teeth, something the bitewing did not capture.

All three types of x-rays were developed in the darkroom. Any dental technician was trained to expose and develop radiographs; however, one of the dental technicians, DN Steve Quick, was appointed to be the official x-ray technician who did most of the radiography work for the ship's clinic.

Also in the x-ray space was the *Central Sterilization Room* (CSR), where contaminated instruments were cleaned, sterilized, and packaged into sealed plastic bags that would keep them sterile for a long time.

In leaving the x-ray room and moving down the passageway just a few feet, you would encounter a space to the right which held two operatory chairs. Prophies were done there. During my first year aboard the USS Kennedy, we had three general dentists. During my second year aboard, an additional general dentist was added to the department and he was to use one of these chairs. During that first year, however, both chairs were used to help keep the crew's teeth clean.

Proceeding down the passageway, you would pass the ladder and waiting room where you originally entered the dental spaces. Continuing down the p-way, on your left, would be first an oral surgery room, then a general dentistry room, and then one more general dentistry room. Each of these contained one operatory chair. On the right, you would have passed the large administrative space and then another general dentistry room. If you extended your arms out fully to your sides, you would be able to touch simultaneously the right and left bulkheads that composed the passageway. At the end of the passageway, straight ahead, was the dental lab.

The oral surgery room held electronic monitoring equipment that included an electrocardiograph, pulse oximeter, and Life-Pak 5 electric shock cardiac stimulator. There were tanks containing nitrogen for use with the Hall handpieces. There was plenty of storage space for the surgical instruments.

The administration room, frequently referred to as "admin," housed the dental charts of all the personnel attached to the ship, a couple computers, several file cabinets containing information such as official instructions and procedure manuals, a clipboard displaying the Plan of the Day, and a TV.

The lab had the equipment necessary to manufacture partial and full dentures, and metal and porcelain-fused-to-metal crowns and bridges. The department coffee machine was set up here, too. There was a model trimmer and a lathe, and there were fans, case pans, and articulators.

All personnel assigned to dental departments aboard U.S. aircraft carriers were active duty members of the United States Navy. At times, reservists would be assigned for a short duration. Two enlisted personnel were experienced dental laboratory technicians, who would make crowns and dentures. The remaining enlisted personnel would serve as administrative clerks, personnel managers, chairside assistants, dental hygienists, x-ray technicians, and maintenance personnel.

When equipment broke, repairs were done by trained repair technicians attached not to the ship but to the homeport naval base. They would make trouble calls to the various ships tied up at the piers. When the ship was away from its homeport and equipment failed, we would have to improvise and rig up our own suitable repair or contact repair personnel in other ports who could rendezvous with the ship at some point. Fortunately, we never required any major repairs that stopped operations.

When at sea, we typically worked four and a half hours each morning, from 0700 to 1130. Lunch would be from 1130 to 1300, the hour-and-a-half duration necessary in order to ensure that all the enlisted personnel would have enough time to move through the long lunch lines on the mess decks. At times, they might have to wallow in line for an hour before getting food. We returned to work from 1300 to 1600 in the afternoon. Then we worked again from 1800 to 2000. We did this every day of the week, except Sunday, when the clinic was closed in the morning. There was always one dental officer and two technicians on call to treat after-hours emergencies.

So now that breakfast was over and I joined the dental staff to begin another workday, we had a brief muster and then began seeing patients. My assistant and I were in the middle of doing an amalgam on one of the ship's barbers when DN Wade Lohmann, one of the dental techs, had to interrupt treatment for a moment when he politely inquired if he could retrieve something he had stored above the clinic's white-painted drop ceiling. Since storage space was at a premium aboard ship, the personnel had to be creative, and many of the techs kept things stored and hidden from view above the drop ceiling.

Music blared from the radio-cassette player in my operatory. Because we were located so deeply within the interior of the massive vessel, radio signals could not be picked up. There was, however, a never-ending supply of cassette tapes that would somehow find their way into my room, provided by the dental crew. They would stop by and say, "Doctor Trently, give this tape a listen . . . see what you think." I enjoyed music, so never hesitated to take up the offer. The range of music styles was incredibly wide. We listened to everything from the Violent Femmes to The Smiths to Frank Zappa, rap, jazz, classical, and country. Some patients even brought their own tapes.

Dental appointments were usually forty-five minutes long. My 0830 appointed patient failed to show up, so I squeezed in a minor emergency and then had a few minutes to climb the ladder out of dental and make my way to the port *sponson*, a small area exposed to the outdoors but covered by an overhead, and situated just a few yards above the water's surface. Petty Officer Pellet was there, gazing out at the sea. This was a great place to watch porpoises swimming and frolicking alongside the ship. I was in luck—there were three of them jumping in formation above the deep blue water. A few flying fish made guest appearances, flashing their silvery reflections as they bounced up out of the sea. During storms, the hatch leading to the sponson would be secured (closed) because waves could crash into the semi-enclosed area.

After a few minutes taking in the salty air, I returned down the ladders to Dental. During the performance of dental treatment, the doctors wore those same yellow smocks I had worn while working ashore at the naval base. The techs wore a sea-green smock.

Not only were the physical surroundings colorful, but also the human beings who inhabited the spaces as patients or staff. One of my patients that morning came in for a routine exam. When I went to do the oral cancer screening exam and lifted his lower lip, I noticed a deviation from normal. The inside of his lower lip was tattooed with an expletive in big bold letters, "F—YOU." He beamed an exuberant smile, like a proud father, as he explained how it hurt "like a son of a gun" when installed.

Another guy that came in that morning was missing a few teeth and, when I asked him if he ever wore a partial denture, he explained calmly how he had one made last year when he was attached to a battleship, but "hated it so much—it never fit right—that I threw it overboard somewhere in the Atlantic."

After seeing a few more patients, we wrapped it up for the morning. I said, "Time to watch some flight ops before I get lunch." I ascended several ladders in the ship's *island*, which is an aircraft carrier's superstructure—the part of the ship that rises above the flight deck. Almost out of breath, I finally reached the observation deck high up in the tower overlooking the flight deck, a place called Vulture's Row.

In order to leave the shelter of the tower to go outdoors to the small area of Vulture's Row, you first had to apply hearing protection—usually simple earplugs—because out there it would get loud. You were also required to remove your cover; a hat could easily be blown off one's head and tumble onto the deck where it could be sucked into an aircraft and cause damage. I used both of my arms as I muscled the heavy latch open, moving onto the open deck of Vulture's Row. About five crewmembers were already there, taking in the sights. The sun was shining and the seas were calm.

There was the usual humming, droning noise. You could feel the intense heat blowing from the aircraft toward your face. The unmistakable smell of JP-4 (jet fuel) dominated, although occasionally your nose might detect the various scents of the open ocean.

Even with earplugs in place it was still very loud up there. The world of the flight deck was an eerie one, where no one talked without shouting, and communication was primarily accomplished by accentuated hand and body gestures.

This was a dangerous place to work. Deck personnel wore safety goggles and hearing protection, their soiled and tattered gloves and clothes flapping in the incessant wind currents crisscrossing the open deck from the sea or from the powerful wind bursts originating from the aircraft. They wore float vests around their waists in case they got blown overboard. Some service members had been sucked into the intake of aircraft. One deckhand recounted how he had seen a man decapitated after he accidentally walked in front of an S-3's intake. Another person was severely injured by a broken cable that whipped out of control. And there was always the danger of getting run over by one of the many vehicles traversing the flight deck. You also had to watch out for the whirring blades of the E-2C Hawkeyes. Personnel attended "P" School, a short course that informed them how to avoid getting killed or maimed while doing their specific jobs on the flight deck.

They were a motley crew, this dedicated bunch of young people, whose average age was nineteen. The young, hard working kids who labored here under a wide range of extreme weather conditions were given great responsibilities. They were in charge of multimillion dollar aircraft. Sloppy work could lead to aircraft and equipment damage. If an aircraft was pushed too far, it could tumble over the edge of the deck into the ocean's depths. Or a plane could crash into another as it was being moved across the deck. Vehicles routinely passed by each other within inches as they were carefully rearranged on the runways with precise and methodical planning and maneuvering. These aviation workers were also responsible for performing regular maintenance, and if they became careless about this it could cost the lives of the pilot and crew.

White wave crests broke up the glassy texture of the ocean. The radars were rapidly turning high above on the tower. Directives blared from the loudspeakers. People hurried back and forth all around the deck. You would at times see heads emerge from sunken openings at the side of the flight deck alongside the peripheral catwalks, then disappear again as the individual stepped down to a lower level.

The flat surface of the flight deck equaled about five acres of land. It was made of steel, covered by a rough, rubber-like coating called *non-skid* that was black in color. There were yellow lines painted to direct flight traffic. White *tie-downs* were metal disks sunk into the deck, spaced about a yard apart, used for securing aircraft. Four thick metal cables were stretched across the deck, used to capture aircraft when they came in for a landing.

If you talked to the flight deck personnel, they would enthusiastically and proudly describe to you what their job involved. They invariably felt good about what they did. Sometimes they worked twelve to eighteen hours a day, often missing a hot meal. Boxed lunches could sometimes be provided. I often nearly stepped on some of these guys as I passed through the long passageways below the flight deck, as they lay on the deck taking a break, trying to catch a few winks.

The flight deck crew wore different colored shirts, each color representing the specific job of its wearer. The Blue Shirts *chocked and chained* the aircraft, which meant they were responsible for securing aircraft to the deck. This was the first job of a Blue Shirt. After gaining experience chocking and chaining, a person would next move up to become a tractor driver, pulling aircraft around the deck. There was a fleet of vehicles travelling around on the deck. Most of these were used to move aircraft and were called *stubbies* or *mules*. There was an enormous movable crane, and an even larger hoist called *Big John* fixed to the ship aft of the island, used to load and unload boats and aircraft when the carrier was berthed. There was the *scrubber*, the equivalent of the machine used to smooth ice rinks. When the mixture of saltwater, JP-4, and other ingredients made the deck too slick for safe landings, the scrubber came in to clean it up.

After gaining experience as a Blue Shirt, you could then become a Yellow Shirt, a person who directed the aircraft traffic on the flight deck so that movement of planes was accomplished quickly and safely.

The Purple Shirts were responsible for refueling the aircraft. They were nicknamed "grapes." There were twenty-six fueling stations on the catwalk that surrounded the flight deck. That was like having twenty-six gas stations aboard.

The Green Shirts were responsible for maintenance and operation of the catapults and arresting gear.

The Brown Shirts were the plane captains who performed the final tweaks on aircraft prior to flight, and who rode in the aircraft as they were moved around the deck, braking when necessary.

The Red Shirts were the firemen and crash and salvage workers and, in addition, were the personnel responsible for storing, transporting, and loading ordnance.

There were always a few folks dressed in fire-retardant shiny silver suits—the "Hot Suit Men"—always ready to move into fiery wreckage with the primary goal of trying to save the lives of the crew.

White Shirts were responsible for quality assurance and safety.

I waited patiently for the flight ops to begin. Most of the aircraft were on the flight deck, many of them with their wings folded to maximize the storage space, their tail ends overlapping the edge of the deck with nothing but the ocean below. Others were being transported up to the flight deck from the hangar deck below by way of the ship's four elevators. Each elevator weighed greater than 130,000 pounds and could carry another 130,000 pounds of load. Each elevator could lift two F-14s the distance of more than forty feet from the hangar deck to the flight deck in less than six seconds. Specific people were assigned to safely coordinate elevator operations. There was also an ordnance elevator near the island, used to bring weapons up to the deck.

Earlier in the morning, the deck crew and any volunteers lined up on the flight deck and marched slowly the entire length of the ship searching for and removing any loose debris. This was called a *FOD walkdown*. Pieces of the non-skid sometimes worked their way loose and, if sucked into the intakes of a jet engine, could cause severe damage. The same applied to any other kind of loose debris.

FOD stood for "Foreign Object Damage." I participated in a FOD walkdown maybe a couple times during my two years on the ship.

At last the F-14 pilots emerged from someplace within the superstructure, wearing the olive green flight suits, striding confidently out to their respective aircraft. After a cursory pre-flight inspection, the pilots nonchalantly climbed into their cockpits, portraying the image of coolness even in the face of imminent danger. It was said that carrier pilots developed an attitude of superiority toward other aircraft pilots. This arose at least partly from the fact that they needed to launch from and land on such a small runway where there was much less room for error.

Naval aviators wore brown shoes to distinguish themselves from the *blackshoes*, who were the officers of ship's company. The pilots tended to be more raucous than the blackshoes. And the F-14 pilots were the most fire-breathing of all the aviators. After all, to do the job that they did, one needed to be more aggressive and wild. Their mission was to chase and kill the enemy in air-to-air combat, a task that required one to live on the edge. And even when not in combat, their mission was dangerous; each year many aircraft mishaps during routine training could be expected as the norm. The nature of the machinery and what needed to be done with that machinery invited dangerous situations.

Navy pilots needed to requalify periodically in survival training. The test was grueling. For example, I was told that one of the requirements was that they had to jump in the water with full flight gear on, have a large parachute fall over them, and then try to escape from under it. They'd have to hold their breath when under the water, push the heavy parachute up when they surfaced to get air, and scramble to find the edge to escape from under it. LT Jack Griffin, a Navy dentist stationed with me back at the Naval Dental Center took the certification test in order to become qualified to ride in the back seat of a catapulted aircraft. He was in excellent physical condition and passed the test, but he said it was a "humbling" experience. He said several of the established pilots taking the test for recertification did not pass. Because of his certification, Jack later was to hitch a ride in Navy aircraft while stationed aboard the USS Roosevelt.

There were many aircraft attached to the Air Wing, each with its own specific job. The first aircraft to leave the flight deck was the Sikorsky SH-3H Sea King helicopter. We called it a *helo*. There were six of these on the carrier. The Sea King's job was antisubmarine warfare, but it was extremely versatile in that it was also used for anti-ship missile defense, surface surveillance, search and rescue, and emergency medevacs. The helicopter, with its crew of two pilots and two aircrewmen, could attack submarines with MK-46 torpedoes from forward flight or from a hover. The reason it was the first aircraft to become airborne was so it would be in a ready position to rescue the pilots and crew of subsequent launches in case they had to eject into the water.

The ship turned its course into the wind. The first aircraft to be launched from a catapult was the E-2C Hawkeye, which provided early detection and warning of approaching enemy forces. The carrier had four of these, and they were nicknamed "hummers" because of the noise they made. They accomplished their mission by using their powerful long-range radar and sophisticated computer-controlled electronic systems. The E-2C Hawkeye was a twin-engine turbo-prop that could attain speeds of three-hundred knots and altitudes of thirty-thousand feet. It had an eighty-foot wingspan and weight of greater than twenty-four tons, and thus was one of the largest aircraft operating from aircraft carriers. The crew consisted of a pilot, co-pilot, combat information center officer, air control officer, and flight technician. Fixed atop this aircraft was a twenty-four foot rotating disk antenna, through which the radar transmitted its energy. The E-2C could usually be spotted next to the island with the helos.

The F-14 Tomcat reigned supreme in aerial maneuverability and dog-fighting capabilities. This was the jet aircraft made famous by the movie, *Top Gun*. Its mission was to intercept and destroy enemy aircraft, in any type of weather, to establish and maintain local air superiority. It reached speeds in excess of Mach 2.0 and was powered by two TF 30-P-412 Turbofan engines equipped with afterburners, each providing over twenty-thousand pounds of thrust. It had a crew of two: a pilot and a flight officer. There were about two dozen of these aircraft on the carrier. Two Tomcats called "Alert Birds" were always parked behind the island, fully armed and fueled, ready to go on five minutes' notice.

The A6 Intruder was the ship's attack bomber. It was subsonic and not maneuverable like the F-14, especially when loaded with ordnance and fuel tanks. But the A6's value lay in its ability to fly long distances at low level, day or night, in the worst of weather, deep into enemy territory with a big bomb load capable of hitting targets with pinpoint accuracy. It had a two-man crew, consisting of pilot and bombardier. There were about twenty Intruders aboard ship. Five of these aircraft equaled one Air Force B-52 bomber. The metal rod jutting out from its front was the housing for the night and bad weather electronics.

Another aircraft was the KA-6D tanker, of which there were four attached to each Intruder squadron. These were a spinoff from the A6 design. They were fitted with fuel hose reels which replaced the night and bad weather bombing electronics housing. This allowed the KA-6D to accomplish its mission, which was to refuel other aircraft while in flight.

Another spinoff from the A6 was the EA-6B Prowler. Its job was to detect and jam enemy radar communications. Modern anti-air defense systems relied heavily on radar for tracking guidance. By denying the enemy the use of his radars, the EA-6B could effectively screen friendly strike aircraft and neutralize enemy weapons systems. So even though the EA-6B did not fire bombs, bullets, or missiles, it was an integral part of the carrier's defense. The crew was made up of four: one pilot and three electronic countermeasure officers. There were about four EA-6Bs in each carrier wing. I was told that just four of these aircraft strategically placed could knock out the entire communication system of the United States.

Also aboard ship was the S-3 Viking which searched for and destroyed enemy submarines, and was described in the Introduction. Its foremost task was to protect the high value target—the aircraft carrier itself. Turbofans gave the Viking the power to push through the thick air of low altitudes, as distinct from the E-2C Hawkeye's twin turboprops that were designed to propel this aircraft through the thinner atmosphere of higher altitudes. The peculiar vacuum-cleaner sound the S-3 made had earned it the nickname, "Hoover." There were ten of these on the carrier.

The COD, acronym for "carrier onboard delivery," was a version of the E-2C Hawkeye with all the electronics removed. Its job was to fly critical parts as well as people onto and off the ship. The mail was also delivered by the COD.

Now that the helos and E-2Cs were airborne, it was time to launch the rest of the aircraft. It usually involved some forty people in the preparation for a cat shot. The ship had four catapults, each of which propelled aircraft off the flight deck from zero miles per hour to one-hundred seventy miles per hour in one-hundred feet and less than two seconds! One aircraft could be launched every thirty seconds on average.

After the F-14 was guided to its launch position and the deck crew hooked the plane to the catapult and all hands were clear, the catapult officer, called "Shooter," held up two fingers and rotated his hand to tell the pilot to rev up his engines. The afterburners opened up and ominous red flames twenty-five feet long and three feet in diameter began roaring backward against the Jet Blast Deflectors (JBD), which had just been hydraulically raised. The JBDs helped restrict the path of the flames, directing them away from the flight deck to protect people and aircraft aft of the launching plane.

As the jet aircraft thundered its full power against the JBD, and the pilot was ready, the pilot saluted the catapult officer, who then saluted back. The cat officer then crouched down and touched the deck with his hand. Then, in a semi-crouch, he thrust his torso, arm, and hand into a forward point. This signaled the catapult operator to slam the palm-size launch button with the flat of his hand. Below the flight deck, a massive valve exploded open, shaking the ship. A great volume of steam delivered a sledgehammer blow to the catapult piston. The cat shot the plane, blowing steam the entire length of its track. You could always, even when you were way below this airport that operated atop the ship, hear and feel the jets rolling across the flight deck during launch as they were hurled into the air.

The whole process was coordinated by the Air Boss in the tower. During busy periods, there could be three-hundred flights per day. The Air Boss needed to make snap decisions. He was connected to all parts of the deck by phone, radio, and loudspeaker.

During wartime, the ship's primary defense was provided by its aircraft. Without the aircraft support, the ship could defend itself by its NATO Sea Sparrow Missile System (NSSMS), of which it had three. It also had three Close-In Weapons Systems (CIWS) which were stationed around the ship providing three-hundred sixty degree defensive coverage. The CIWS was a radar-controlled twenty millimeter Gatling gun capable of firing at a rate of three-thousand rounds per minute. Altogether, it was mind-boggling to know that the ship had more firepower than was used during all the military engagements of World War Two.

I watched a few landings. The aircraft lowered their tailhooks as they approached the ship. The pilot aimed for, ideally, the third of four greasy, one-and-one-half inch thick diameter metal cables that were stretched across the deck in the aft part of the ship. The planes came toward the ship with a pronounced tail-down attitude, speed brakes on full, engines at seventy-five percent power, air speed as high as one-hundred forty knots, dropping fast. They appeared to waver unsteadily as they made the approach. Then they slammed onto the deck in a "controlled crash" with fifty to eighty tons of impact—many times that of a commercial airliner on a concrete runway. This made a tremendous noise. Fine droplets of oil and grease were flung everywhere, spraying the men standing nearby.

If the tailhook had missed the cable, the pilot would have had three seconds to get the speed brakes retracted before being able to fly again off the deck and back up into the air, to try again to land later. A failed landing attempt was called a *bolter*.

The arresting cables were checked carefully each day for defects. A worn cable could snap in two under the stress and whip around the deck, causing death and injury. Whenever flaws were detected, the cable was removed and thrown overboard.

With a successful "trap," the pilot then followed the expert guidance of a director in a yellow jersey to swiftly get his aircraft off the landing runway before the next aircraft arrived. He folded his wings, gently gunned the jets, and steered where directed, as part of the well-coordinated master plan. Then his "bird" was tied down to the deck with chains. The pilot then got out of the aircraft, climbed down from the cockpit, and headed to a debriefing in the intelligence center. This debriefing was extremely important because flight plans immediately following could depend on what he saw and did.

It was time to leave Vulture's Row, to get some lunch. After working in patients' mouths all morning, manipulating small instruments into tiny spaces, meticulously scrutinizing every move of the high-speed handpiece, and worrying about pulp protection and which cusps to cap over, the flight deck put it all into perspective. It was good to refocus the eyes and take a break from fighting the battles in the dental trenches to see what other people had to do for work each day. Up here, the world opened up. It was boundless as I looked out over the ocean's curved horizon. Up here, you got a bigger picture. It was a reminder that there was more to life than just dentistry. I now felt invigorated and ready to return below.

I began to exit Vulture's Row, but then paused and turned around to look back one more time at all the action. The thought occurred to me that it was here on the flight deck where you could more directly observe the results of all the efforts at trying to keep dental readiness high (of course, along with the hard work of all the other occupations represented aboard the ship, from the cooks and barbers to the engineers and chaplains, as these groups labored to do the things they did to achieve the overall mission). The seemingly small things we did below to try to keep the crew healthy contributed to what went on up here. I was beginning to understand what the C.O. of the Naval Dental Center meant when he said we were officers first, and dentists second. There was a bigger picture.

I found an empty seat in the wardroom and reserved it for myself by crossing the silverware into an "X" in the place where the plate would go. This was the accepted sign understood by the ship's officers. Then I moved through the lunch line to get food.

Returning to the long dining table that sat perhaps ten people, I noticed I was sitting next to the navigator, a lawyer, an engineer, and the Bull Ensign. "How you doing, Doc?" they greeted me with as I took a seat. They continued their preexisting conversation that had begun before I arrived. Listening attentively, I swore they spoke a foreign language, filled as it was with Navy acronyms and technical jargon. "That needed to be promulgated in accordance with the HSG, but the message traffic did not forward the RStars. So if you look at the OPPE, you'd see they never met with the JTF the other day. CommO decided to send W/C 620 a 7-3T during RAS ASAP!" I just thought to myself, *Huh? What up with that?*

At 1300 we began seeing patients again. Doc Wallace had to ground a pilot, to the pilot's dismay, because local anesthetic had been used in a dental procedure. Aviators did not like to miss flight time. The guidelines said a twenty-four hour grounding was required for the protection of the pilot and the aircraft. Wouldn't want him flying erratically while under the influence of lidocaine. Lucky for the pilot that he did not undergo root canal therapy, for which he would have been grounded for seventy-two hours.

To ground a pilot, we had to fill out a *chit*, which was Navy talk for a request form used in everyday transactions. The first time I heard the word repeatedly mentioned, I just had to ask, "Excuse me? What the heck is a 'chit,' or whatever it was that you just said?"

As my assistant and I were affixing a matrix band to our patient's tooth, Petty Officer Marvin Gordon from Detroit entered the room to vent his frustrations about the world. We nonchalantly continued to work meticulously on the patient as we listened, enjoying the entertainment. Following a five-minute bombastic diatribe condemning the arms race or some such subject, arms flailing all around as he tried to emphasize various points, he felt better and began to return quietly to the lab to work on a denture framework he was casting for one of LCDR Wallace's patients. "Thanks for letting me vent, Doc," he said calmly as he left the room. The patient just smiled in amusement, as best he could while his mouth was stuffed with cotton rolls and a saliva ejector and a retainer sticking out over his lower lip.

We completed filling the patient's tooth and gave him the usual post-op instructions. Most of the time aboard an aircraft carrier you could feel the deck moving as the ship pitched and rolled in the ocean, but the undulations were subtle for the most part. If you were aboard a small ship like a destroyer, the movement would catch much more of your attention. On a carrier, there were occasions, however, when this movement could be severe when the seas were particularly rough. You could find yourself to be physically nudged, albeit gently, from one side of a passageway to the other by the shifting deck if you were not paying attention to maintaining your balance. A few times when the JFK was caught in fierce storms with forty-foot waves, the deck moved a lot and the practice of dentistry became difficult. One day I had to rush through a patient's treatment so I could retire to my stateroom rack before getting overly seasick. At moments like these, we passed the word to secure loose items, like the x-ray tube head, to prevent damage.

DT3 Derrick McCorey came by the room to give me five patient charts to review as part of the quality assurance program. On a regular basis, dental personnel did this, looking for improper chart entries and treatment discrepancies. It was a way to watch out for negative trends by providers that might need to be addressed and modified.

DT3 McCorey was from the inner city streets of Philadelphia. He told me that he joined the Navy in order to escape from the rampant drug scene that was surrounding everybody he knew from there. I thought to myself, "Good for you. At least you didn't just give up and do like so many others."

Suddenly it was announced that there was a mercury spill in AIMD. Since I was the ship's Mercury Control Officer (MCO), I grabbed the Mercury Spill Kit and my assistant, and rushed to the site of the catastrophe. Tongue in cheek, we did it up big time, like the Ghost Busters. Often, I sent one of our trained technicians, but that day I wanted to personally oversee the damage.

It took about ten minutes to traverse the ship's passageways to AIMD. Upon arrival at the spill site, we surveyed the area. If cleanup could not be effectively accomplished by us, or if other substances in addition to mercury were involved, or if there was the existence of or potential for dangerous conditions that we could not handle effectively, we were to immediately contact the Duty Fire Marshall or Duty Engineer for assistance. This particular spill involved less than two ounces of mercury, considered a very small and relatively harmless quantity when discarded in the proper manner. The Dental Department Mercury Spill Cleanup Squad could successfully handle this case.

The spill occurred in 02-99-5-Q, the AIMD Cal Lab. AT1 Farmer noticed a broken Hg (chemical symbol for mercury) thermometer and reported it to AT1 Shaffer, who then called the Dental Department and AIMD Quality Assurance Officer. ATC Tyson of AIMD surmised the cause of the shattering to be from the stress of the ship vibration and shocks of aircraft launched, and considered this to be an isolated incident not likely to be repeated once a simple relocation of the affected equipment was effected.

For the moment, however, the Cleanup Squad had a job to do. All personnel not involved in the operation were instructed to avoid the area. A boundary delineating contaminated from noncontaminated areas was identified, with a safety buffer zone of ten feet extended beyond the contaminated area. Smoking, eating, and drinking were prohibited within this zone due to the potential for inhalation or ingestion of toxic mercury. Mercury vaporized at room temperature and had no odor or color. Once Hg entered the body, it concentrated in the liver, brain, and kidney, and was excreted at a slow rate. Prolonged excessive exposure was dangerous because it could lead to central nervous system disorders, severe psychological disturbances, and various physiological problems. A single short-duration exposure would not cause severe problems, but if the spill was not cleaned up prolonged exposure could cause problems.

Traffic was redirected away from the area of contamination. Legible, easily-recognized signs notifying personnel of the hazard were displayed around the contaminated area. We donned our neoprene gloves, safety goggles, and facemasks. When mercury escaped from its enclosure, it turned into a shiny silver globule that rolled around and, if touched with the right degree of force, divided into multiple smaller droplet spheres. Using an aspirator, we were able to capture the larger globules. To apprehend the smaller droplets, we used our official gear to sweep them into larger masses. If the spill was larger or in a confined space, we had access to and could utilize positive-pressure air respirators and plastic-coated overalls. We also had a Mervac for occasions of larger quantity.

After gross removal, affected surfaces, including our gear, were scrubbed with HgX, a metallic-mercury sulfide converting solution, allowed to dry, and then swabbed with soap and water. Fortunately, this spill did not involve Hg getting trapped within deep narrow surface cracks and crevices, which would have necessitated application of HgX with sawdust to absorb it overnight, followed by sweeping and swabbing the next day.

The retrieved specimens were stored in a double-layered, sealed plastic bag that was placed inside an appropriately-labeled rigid container. This was kept in the dental spaces until which time that it could be removed from the ship and disposed of as directed by the Kennedy's HazMat Officer. I declared the space safe again for normal use and returned to Dental. Over the next few days, I would have to generate a report to the Commanding Officer, identifying what happened and what was done to rectify the discrepancy.

For the moment, however, it was back to dentistry. Our patient required a root canal on tooth #8. An hour later, we obturated the canal and I sent the patient on his way while my assistant turned over the room so we could do an MODL amalgam on the next patient.

Earlier in the day yesterday, my assistant and I extracted a tooth on a young sailor who had had a severe infection and experienced excessive bleeding post-operatively. We took extra measures to get him stabilized enough to be able to dismiss him, but told him to let us know how he was doing later in the day. He had not shown up or called by the stated time, so we contacted his department and his division officer said he was indeed ordered to report back to us. Now a day later, after we called his department again, the patient finally showed up. When I asked him why he didn't follow the instructions, he just gave some wishy-washy response that amounted to, "Well, I just didn't feel like it." Obviously this person needed to be impressed with the seriousness of this situation, so I proceeded to instruct him loudly and then, for emphasis, took my provider chair and hurled it across the deck so it slammed into the opposite bulkhead. That seemed to get his attention. When I subsequently took a look intraorally, I observed that he was healing within normal limits and so I noted that in his chart. As he departed the room, I delicately rolled my chair back to its normal position and chuckled quietly to myself.

Over the 1-MC we heard the message, "Sweepers, sweepers, man your brooms. Give the ship a clean sweep down fore and aft." Periodically during the day this announcement was piped by the boatswain's mate of the watch, and was the signal to all men assigned as sweepers to draw their gear and sweep and swab their assigned spaces, and empty all trash receptacles.

At 1600 we wrapped it up in Dental. I headed to my stateroom to change into workout clothes, and then hustled over to the forward gym, one of two gyms aboard the ship. After stretching, I lifted weights on the universal press. There were about twenty of the ship's crew working out. Some used the free weights. I rode one of several stationary bikes, listening to music on headphones. Closing my eyes, I tried to imagine myself cycling through some scenic area ashore.

This evening was my night to eat dinner with the XO (ship's Executive Officer, the second in command). About fifteen officers from various departments were in attendance as well. As the ship plowed along through the ocean, we dined in a separate room within the wardroom. Dinner was served by a team of waiters. Candles illuminated the table. This was a change of pace from dining in the main part of the wardroom, where we served ourselves and did not have candlelight dining. The XO periodically scheduled these special meals in order to spark conversation with his officers to learn more about them and how they were doing running the ship. After dessert, we were served coffee. The XO required us to come prepared with a trivia question. One by one, we took turns going around the table presenting a question from any topic, which ranged therefore from Bugs Bunny cartoons to nautical history and so on. The XO would attempt to answer first or he would ask for help around the table.

After dinner, at 1800 (6:00 PM), it was time to go back to Dental. Usually in the evening we did T2 exams, sometimes as many as twenty or more apiece. We also held sick call. The techs took necessary x-rays, and developed, mounted, and labeled them. They took blood pressures and updated the paperwork, including the health questionnaires.

"Mail Call. That is, Mail Call," was announced throughout the ship. Everybody loved to hear those words. It was not every day that we received postage while away at sea. We sent our runner to the post office aft and waited anxiously for him to return with a huge canvas bag, feeling perhaps a bit like Santa Claus. It took a while for him to return and when he did, the sack was full but gradually emptied as individual stamped envelopes were passed out to the lucky addressees. Occasionally, cardboard boxes of food from home—like chocolate-chip cookies—or supplies unavailable out here arrived. If someone got cookies, it would only be a matter of minutes for the sailor sharks to devour the whole box.

I just finished an exam when general quarters was sounded. "General Quarters! General Quarters! All hands man your Battle Stations! This is a drill! This is a drill!" Our patients would have to come back another time. Personnel immediately headed to their GQ battle stations. Traffic flow was orderly. Personnel on the port side of the ship could only move aft and down, while personnel on the starboard side could only move forward and up. My GQ station was the Aft Auxilliary BDS (Battle Dressing Station), just below the flight deck. Starting from the Dental Department, which was on the port side, I had to cross over to starboard, climb up several ladders to the O-3 level, cross to the port side, and then travel aft to the BDS.

The ship had five battle dressing stations. Each was a medical center. They were located far apart from each other so that the ship would not lose all its medical capabilities from one single enemy missile explosion. One BDS was inside the ship's superstructure and was designed to provide care to injured aircrewmen swiftly after they were removed from their aircraft on the flight deck. Two battle dressing stations were located just below the flight deck—one of these at the forward end and the other at the aft end of the flight deck (my BDS, Aft Aux, was one of these). The other two BDSs were located deep inside the ship in more protected areas. Dental officers were usually assigned as officers-in-charge of two of the five stations. There were about eight personnel assigned to my BDS. Our function was to provide first aid to casualties during combat and during peacetime catastrophes such as aircraft crashes and flight deck fires.

We wore flash shields covering our head and neck to protect from flames. Over these were very heavy and thick steel combat helmets to guard against head trauma. We fastened inflatable life preservers around the waist; this "fanny pack" also contained a dye which could be released into the water to enable searchers to find you more easily in the boundless ocean, and a flashlight and whistle. We had to tuck our pant legs inside our socks, to prevent our pants from getting snagged on protruding objects during combat situations.

One designated person from the BDS manned the phone. He would keep in contact with Damage Control Central, which would tell him what routes were safe in case we had to transport casualties to Main Medical. Damage Control Central was constantly fed data about what areas of the ship were on fire, flooded, or destroyed.

We practiced litter carries during GQ. As we discovered, transporting casualties from one part of a ship to another, having to negotiate turns in its narrow passageways and up and down its ladders, was extremely difficult. We used Neil-Robertson stretchers, which allowed us to remove a casualty from engine room spaces, holes, and other compartments where access hatches were too small to permit the use of a regular stretcher. It was constructed of semi-rigid canvas and was wrapped around the casualty in mummy-fashion. The litter most commonly used for transporting casualties was the Stokes stretcher, which was a wire basket supported by iron or aluminum rods. It could be adapted for a variety of uses since the victim could be held securely in place even if the stretcher had to be tipped or turned.

We held incessant training on how to set up IV's, load syringes, establish airways, obtain and record vital signs, and how to perform other combat casualty medical procedures. During training, *floppers* would drop by. These were crewmembers dressed in moulage to simulate certain kinds of injuries, such as a sucking chest wound. They would scream and hurl themselves into the bulkhead to announce their arrival, and we had to assess and treat their injuries. In fact, everyone on the ship had to at least know the first aid for any of the *GITMO 5 wounds*: abdominal and protruding intestine, hand amputation, head wound, sucking chest wound, and compound fracture of the leg.

We had a deck of cards, each card listing a piece of equipment, drug, or instrument stored in the BDS. One by one we drew the cards and had to locate the item within thirty seconds, another skill essential in an emergency situation. The Head Corpsman was responsible for maintaining a current inventory of all supplies, replacing expired drugs at the appropriate time. He also had to monitor our emergency supply of potable water, regularly testing it for bacterial growth.

We had to don gas masks and properly test them whenever chemical warfare was involved. Personnel had to know how to use the autoclave and chemical sterilization supplies. We had to know how to use the overhead surgery light and battle lanterns. We needed to know where the *EEBD*s (emergency egress breathing devices) were located and their proper usage. These were slipped over the head and tightened around the neck, with an oxygen cartridge hanging to the rear, providing a few minutes' worth of oxygen for you to breathe if trapped in a fire, enough to allow you to move into a safe place.

General Quarters could last anywhere from one to several hours. This evening it was called off after only one hour. "Secure from General Quarters!" was announced. We removed our gear and stowed it neatly. I completed the log entry and returned to

Dental. By now it was 2000 (8:00 PM) and there were no dental emergencies.

I made a run to the ship's store, located on the second deck, where I purchased a few needed items like soap and envelopes. I browsed through the aisles to see if there were any new Navy t-shirt or sweatshirt designs. Some uniform items were also available.

From there I traveled to the library, located far aft and a long hike along the second deck. The second deck was the ship's equivalent of a "Main Street" in this floating city. I passed through several mess decks. Opening the door to the library, I entered that quiet haven, discovering about a dozen sailors sitting at the tables. A few more were standing and browsing in the narrow rows of bookshelves, each shelf designed with a lip on its edge in case books shifted during the ship's unpredictable movements. The library was open until midnight. Newspapers hung neatly against one bulkhead. There were also several rows of shelves holding a wide assortment of books, which I often browsed through, reading some of them in their entirety. There was a collection of old cruisebooks, each bound volume commemorating a major deployment aboard the USS Kennedy. There were photos of the crews and ports visited. It was interesting to note that most of the cruisebooks had an "In Memoriam" page that listed the names of crewmembers who had passed away during that deployment, most of them pilots. It was amusing to see pictures of bearded sailors from older deployments in the days when more facial hair was permitted.

I took a seat and finished an administrative project I had been working on. I had brought from home a few paperbacks which I sometimes read in the library, but this night I did not bring any with me. Instead, I read information about upcoming tours when the ship would anchor in various ports.

At 2130 I departed the library and went to a secluded place near the *fantail* (rear) of the ship, a place where one could take in magnificent views of the ocean. Two of the medical officers were there. I joined them, swapping stories of what transpired at general quarters. The air was filled with a cool breeze that felt refreshing. The ocean's surface was wild with large swells and we could feel saltwater spraying onto our faces as the waves crashed into the hull. Only one ship could be seen on the horizon, its lights flashing periodically in the distance. We wondered what kind of vessel it was, and what people were aboard. Below us, floating near the water's surface, were strange glow-in-the-dark creatures. They looked like stars in the sky on a cloudless night, only they were down below in the water. The ship's anesthesiologist summed up the moment accurately when he proclaimed, "Yeah, this is what it's all about!" I could not have said it any better.

I wondered what it would have been like in the days of wooden ships, like the USS Constitution, to be at sea. You would not hear the same noises as we now experienced. Instead, you would hear the sounds of wood creaking, riding over the waves. It would have been quieter. I wondered what dentistry would have been like in those years.

We decided to check out some night ops at Vulture's Row, so we began the long journey up the ship's island. Once there at Vulture's Row, we joined several other interested shipmates. We were just in time to watch the F-14s being launched. The jet blast deflectors were raised as the massive red flames poured out of the aircraft's afterburners. The sight was more impressive and dramatic at night in the dark, as the flames secondarily illuminated the surrounding air over the flight deck, burning brilliantly behind the aircraft. To witness this was an eerie experience. Then, with a mighty surge forward, the catapult hurled the jet aircraft forward over the edge of the deck into the pitch-black sky. Once airborne for a few seconds, the flames were extinguished and all we saw were a couple taillights from the F-14 slowly disappear into the distance. White puffs of steam dissipated along the deck and we could feel the heat from the next F-14 to be launched. The smell of the jet fuel pervaded the air. Light wands were waved by flight deck personnel to direct the traffic.

After the launches were completed, we headed back down the ladders. I stopped by the wardroom, where some of the officers were stuffing themselves with popcorn and engaging in salty conversation. Some were in the TV lounge watching a movie on the ship's TV channel. I stayed for a while, joining in the popcorn feast, and then returned to my stateroom to retire for the night.

I climbed up to my rack. Lying down on my back, gazing at the metal cables and wires fixed to the overhead not far above my face, I could feel the ship moving up and down, rocking me to sleep. The chaplain's voice came over the 1MC as he recited the evening prayer in a nondenominational way. After that, I extinguished my reading light. Another day at sea was ending.

PART FOUR

FOREIGN SHORES

After leaving the United States and crossing the Atlantic Ocean, we navigated through the Strait of Gibraltar to enter the Mediterranean Sea. As the British sailors say, we "had come across the pond."

I was sitting in my DOR, arranging burs or something, when Petty Officer Ramos walked in and announced in his heavy Puerto Rican accent, "Land ho! Lieutenant, get a good view of Italy!" Hearing "Land ho," I immediately felt like I was a part of some old-time seafaring expedition. We had not seen any solid ground for weeks since we departed Norfolk. "There's land on the horizon!" DT3 Ramos continued.

Several of us from Dental made our way to the starboard catwalk. The ship was passing through the Strait of Messina, between Sicily and mainland Italy. My heart pounded in excitement when I saw the coastline of Italy, which was actually not far away at all—we could see detailed activity ashore from our vantage point aboard our seagoing vessel. To me, this was not just ordinary land. This was "foreign" land, the first time I had seen a country other than the United States or Canada. The view was spectacular. It was evening and the sky was darkening. A myriad of lights from cars, street lights, and buildings dotted the terrestrial landscape. The roads and buildings were situated among the niches of a mountainous terrain. The highways were busy. Slowly the ship continued along the coast. In a day or so we would arrive at our first port of call.

On August 20, 1988 the Kennedy anchored in the Bay of Naples, Italy. Unlike smaller ships such as destroyers, an aircraft carrier could not pull up to the side of most piers but had to remain a distance away where the water was deep. Otherwise, it would run aground. Throughout the entire Med Cruise we had to remain away from any wharves, with the exception of Marseilles, France, where the water was deep enough to harbor us pierside.

To get to shore, you had to wait in line to board a smaller boat which in turn would convey you to *fleet landing*, the name given to the drop-off point ashore. Ferryboats that could transport about two-hundred fifty people at a time were commonly used. A large flat floating metal platform called a *camel* was positioned at the fantail. Ferryboats would pull alongside this. Each sailor would have to step first from the ship to the camel by means of a ladder, and then from the camel onto the ferryboat by stepping across a one to two foot gap where the water lurked below. This created a potentially dangerous situation, as Doctor Terrence Riley explained in *Ship's Doctor*: "If the water was choppy, there were opportunities for falling, spraining an ankle, or getting stuck between objects, both where the ladder from the fantail came to the camel and where the camel abutted the ferryboat. The last of these was the most hazardous because both the camel and the ferryboat would have reciprocal movements. By going opposite directions, they doubled the height of the waves. The camel went down eighteen inches and the ferryboat went up eighteen inches, all in a split second, like a man-sized mousetrap. That was the cause of an occasional laceration, so I had some suturing to do on shins and wrists as the evening wore on and people came and went." During the Med Cruise, I witnessed times when the water was calm but also other moments when it was rough, which did make it interesting getting to that small boat or returning to the aircraft carrier.

The first evening in Naples I went ashore with the chief "to have a real Italian pizza," as he declared. Eating in a restaurant in Italy was a very different experience from the faster pace of American eateries. In Italy it was considered a pleasant pastime when one was able to slow down, relax and enjoy the company one was in while engaging in repast. Eating out in Italy could take anywhere from a half hour to three hours; you were to set your own pace and the waiters did not hassle you to move. The most popular dining hours were from 8:00-10:00 PM.

According to information disseminated from the ship, there were four types of eateries. The first was a ristorante, which was a restaurant in the American sense of three-course meal and drinks. The second was a trattoria, which served home-style meals at low prices. The third was a tavola calda, which was a counter service restaurant, a good place to eat if you did not have much time. The fourth was a pizzeria, where the specialty was, of course, pizza.

Another day, I explored the city by myself. Along the waterfront were large boulders where I found a comfortable spot to read a paperback and get some sun. A few people occupied other rocks, as well as a few cats, minding their own business. The view of the bay was fabulous. Old stone buildings, stuccoed in varying shades of brown or white, lined the waterfront. I could not help but admire their ornate balconies, some of concrete, others black wrought metal. Various arrangements of Doric, Ionic, and Corinthian columns were present. There was a huge castle called Maschio Angioino and public square nearby, and so many embellished buildings with detailed carvings and intricate patterns adorning the facades. It was an architectural delight. Waves splashed onto the boulders below me. Scuba divers submerged in an isolated cove of the inlet.

I walked the road along the bay. Street vendors sold juice, beer, and food. Around the bend of the seaside sidewalk was a thin peninsula that led to an old castle-like structure.

Continuing along the sidewalk, I arrived at a beautiful tree-filled park with an outdoor café where I sat for a while to watch the people and listen to music performed by a singer who accompanied himself on a keyboard wired up to an amplifier and small speakers. Palm trees abounded with acorn-like structures nestled where the limbs branched out from the trunk. Looking up above the treetops, I could discern houses and other building structures arranged in a random, scattered pattern upon a higher elevation.

I returned to the waterfront boulders. The city lay in the shadow of Mount Vesuvius, the historic volcano that erupted in 79 A.D., hurling lava and ash to bury the ancient cities of Pompeii and Herculaneum. I looked out toward the water to see the USS Kennedy anchored in the Bay of Naples, with the quiescent volcano hovering in the distance beyond. What an impressive sight. The ship's aircraft were silent, with their wings folded as they filled the flight deck in their positions of rest.

Naples was the second largest port and third largest city of Italy, with a population of over one million. This was the city of Fellini, Verdi, Rossini, and Puccini. It had given the world the great opera singer Caruso. It was said this incredible city was unlike any other city in Italy, and Neapolitans were unlike any other single group of Italians. The Neapolitan was said to have a reputation for exuberance, sentimentality, and shrewdness. Founded around 600 B.C. by the Greeks, the city later passed to the Romans. I think I got all this information from either a book I read in the ship's library prior to our arrival or from the information put out by the ship's Special Services office.

Stores closed for siesta from 1300-1600, then reopened until 2000. Naples was well-known for its cameos and ceramics. Popular shopping areas were the Piazza Dei Martini and Via Galabritto, all within a short walking distance of fleet landing.

I ambled through narrow streets lined by more old, beautiful buildings. One guy tried to swap my watch for one of about two dozen "Rolexes" he had mounted for display on the inside lining of his trench coat. I politely exited the scene.

In the evening darkness I hiked by myself, exploring more of the city. Naples was a large city, reminiscent of urban places I passed through in the States. There was the noise, the lights, the people, the hustle, and incessant activity. Americans who were stationed there for a long-term tour of duty dubbed it "the armpit of the world," because of their frustrations with the aggressive drivers, crime, and an "everything could wait until tomorrow" attitude among local repairmen and service personnel. During my sojourn I just took it all in stride.

I hiked up a steadily ascending main avenue, away from the waterfront. Bumming a cigarette from some guy hanging out on a street corner, I noticed he wore the loafer shoes and dress pants that most of the Neapolitan males seemed to prefer. These stood in stark contrast to the typical garb of us Americans—jeans, tee shirts, and tennis shoes.

Continuing walking, I passed apartments and a long stretch of row houses. It was dark and some windows were lit up. Inhabitants were dining, drinking, or reading newspapers. Frequently I spotted religious statues and pictures of ancestors displayed in windows. The air smelled of damp soil and there were stone tunnel-like structures that led into what seemed to be central patios. I was not certain.

On the way back to the ship, I discovered an espresso bar and had a cappuccino. During our stay in the Mediterranean we would see more of these European-style coffees in Spain and France. Incidentally, the USS Kennedy had an espresso maker in the wardroom to be used by anyone who knew how to make it work. Only on rare occasions would I hear the sounds of the steam releasing from the machine as someone ventured to use it.

I departed the café and proceeded on, pausing to chat briefly—with some difficulty due to the language barrier—with a burly Austrian woman who seemed very nice. Eventually arriving at fleet landing, I took the ferry back to the ship. All in all, it was an interesting stroll through the city.

Back aboard the ship we had to have a dentist on call at all times to handle any emergencies, so we arranged a schedule in which each dental officer would have duty every fourth day. During this day of duty, he would also see scheduled patients.

One evening when I had the duty, I sauntered around the flight deck after having pounded out a solid day of dentistry. To see the American flag on the ship's stern waving in the breeze, with the coast of Italy as a backdrop, was a moment to remember forever. I felt a strong sense of camaraderie with the rest of the ship's crew. There we were, stuck in some remote corner of the world, away from family and friends, representing the United States as we patrolled the seas ready to protect American interests. We aboard the ship were all in this together and it felt good to be an American.

One of the tours sponsored by JFK's Special Services office was to the resort island of Ischia, an hour's boat ride from Naples. I went with LT Mark Rongone of Dental and LT Bill Sanford, one of the Weapons Department officers. For only $52 we went on a two-day tour of this island, which included the round trip ferry, hotel, dinner, and breakfast. Throughout the deployment, Special Services would offer many exceptional tours at great prices.

The hotel on Ischia was very different from the typical American hotels I had stayed at before. I essentially had a little villa flat, a stand-alone structure, all to myself in the back of this sprawling "hotel," which more resembled a miniature rustic village than the boring, symmetrically-arranged Holiday Inns and Howard Johnsons to which we were accustomed. The landscaping was gorgeous, with bountiful variegated plants and terraced levels and cobblestone walkways, occasional lizards scurrying about. Verdant mountains and volcanoes surrounded us. There were two outdoor saltwater swimming pools and one heated mineral water pool owning an incongruous shape, resembling a winding river as it twisted with trees and shrubs lining its banks.

The weather was hot and sunny. We spent some time at the pools, but also headed for the beaches. One beach was heavily occupied with sunbathers. The "sand" was more like gravel than sand. Another beach was composed of broad flat rocks situated at varying angled orientations and heights, sunners lying atop several of them. Other beaches had real white sand. One resembled a large ashtray because of the unfortunate prevalence of discarded cigarette butts so nonchalantly abandoned by the vacationers. There were many colorful boats. An enormous castle sat in the distance to our right. Beach homes were light-colored in various pastel shades, crumbling with peeling paint, and decorated with all kinds of laundry casually hanging out to dry on clotheslines. The mountain highlands surrounding the beaches added a pretty contrast to the shoreline lowlands.

The whole island had "a lot of character," we agreed. Before leaving, we strolled through the shopping district, which was adorned with narrow, stone-paved streets lined with small shops. We stopped at a rather spacious outdoor bar located in a jungle-like setting, where tables were successfully isolated from each other by large trees and bushes. Waitresses traversed the dirt paths to take orders. Many families were eating ice cream. Little children, old grandmothers, and strollers abounded.

During the boat ride back to Naples we got caught in a severe storm. Four inches of water kept rolling from one side of the boat to the other as it pitched violently from starboard to port. Most of the passengers fled below decks, but most of the Navy sailors remained topside. The spray of water on our faces felt great. Some of the enlisted guys began singing the theme to *Gilligan's Island*, followed by *the Brady Bunch*. Little babies clung tenaciously to their mothers, who tried gallantly to prevent them from getting wet. The rain poured, lightning flashed. Some passengers developed acute seasickness. Then, a turbulent hour later, we made it safely to port and the storm ceased.

A 5K (five kilometers) run was held at Admiral Carney Recreation Park in the outskirts of Naples. The park was situated right in the mouth of an old volcano. In this spacious recreation playground of ninety-six acres and ten baseball fields and other sports facilities, we stretched out and ran the 5K, earning in the process a T-shirt that said *JFK Med Cruise Runs 88-89* on the back and *Italy* and *USS John F. Kennedy* on the front. Throughout the Med Cruise, similar 5K runs were held in other ports. The park was used by armed forces of all the NATO countries stationed in the Naples area. After the run, which involved perhaps a hundred participants from the Kennedy, the dental people got together, sweating profusely and gradually recovering from running over three miles. We bought food and drinks and had our own picnic.

We left Naples on the twenty-seventh of August and would spend the next two days at sea, heading southeast. On the 30th we set anchor at Alexandria, Egypt, where we would remain until the 4th of September.

Alexandria was called the "Pearl of the Mediterranean" and was once the intellectual and cultural center of Greco-Roman civilization. The city of four million people was named after Alexander the Great, who conquered Egypt in 332 B.C.

Several inexpensive tours were arranged by Special Services. There were one-day and two-day tours of Cairo. There was a fifteen-dollar tour of Cairo's El Azhar Mosque, over one-thousand years old, followed by trips to two other mosques and the Islamic Art Museum. There was a twelve-dollar tour to El-Alamein, site of the famous World War Two battle between the forces of Rommel and Montgomery. And there was a $7.50 tour of Alexandria to see the Greco-Roman Museum, Pompey's Pillar, early Christian catacombs, and the Montzah Palace, the residence of King Faruh.

The boat ride from the ship to fleet landing was a long thirty-five minutes on choppy seas, great conditions for inviting seasickness. However, the views of the harbor and especially the sight of the USS Kennedy were worth every minute of it. As the tiny, rocking boat ferried us toward shore, and we gradually moved farther away from the massive floating city we called home, we were able to get a look at the aircraft carrier from several very different, impressive angles.

Once ashore, I tried to walk around by myself as I had done in Naples, but was swarmed upon by street vendors. As I would later discover, most of our stops along the Med had street vendors whom we called "Hey Joes." But none were as persistent as the ones in Egypt. Some of them would try to sell you, for example, headwear called a kufiya (a square of fabric called a ghoutra which was folded and held in place by a circlet of material called an agal) and, if you refused to buy, would actually place it directly on your head and stick out their hand, expecting you to pay up. If you tried to return the merchandise, they would not take it back, but would persist in demanding payment. Then if you dropped the item to the ground in frustration as you walked away, they would pick it up and start all over again. It was best to travel in groups in Egypt in order to more successfully ward them off. This was only a general rule, however, since the ship's MAO (Medical Administration Officer) was an exception: he was able to wander all over Alexandria by himself, enjoying himself immensely as he travelled relatively unimpeded, eventually ending up crawling on his knees blending in with local worshipping Muslims at a mosque. I don't know what his secret was. Maybe he bought one of those headbands on the street right off the bat and the townsfolk immediately rewarded him with friend status and left him alone?

Alexandria's seafront was lined with palm trees, old homes, and modern hotels. At one point along the seaside boulevard, there once stood the Lighthouse of the Pharos, one of the Seven Wonders of the Ancient World. Egypt was one of the world's oldest continuous civilizations, extending back to even before 5000 B.C.

The people of Egypt spoke Arabic. While still aboard the ship, we were taught key Arabic words to assist us in our communication once ashore. A museum was a mat-haf. "Thank you" was Mutta Shakker. "Yes" was aywa. If we had difficulty using Arabic words, or experienced a hard time futilely attempting to pronounce these phonetic spellings I just gave you, it was good to know that most Egyptians spoke English too. Islam was the official religion and over ninety percent of the population was Muslim.

To shop in Egypt, you mostly engaged in bargaining, which was to be conducted in the manner of sport, with its own rules and rewards. It combined the ability to maneuver with the power to persuade, as potential buyers haggled with merchants.

I took the $47 two-day tour of Cairo. Participants packed ourselves into a bus and made the one-hundred ten mile trek over the desert from Alexandria to Cairo. The land was arid most of the way, but one long stretch was filled with green vegetation, where crops such as sugarcane, tomatoes, cotton, watermelons, oranges, rice, corn, and dates grew well. Our tour guide explained how Egyptians were experimenting with various methods of irrigation which were proving to be highly successful in this North African nation.

Much of Cairo looked very modern. We travelled through some impoverished areas. There were exotic street scenes, very different from what you would see in America. As we drove through the city, I saw large pieces of meat hanging outside of shops, in the open air.

Old men smoked from water pipes as they sat on the sidewalks or on chairs outside of the shops. Many of them sipped tea or coffee. Women wore long black garments, often with hoods covering their hair. Huge loaves of bread sat in display outside the bakeshops. The Nile River lay under us as we crossed over a bridge. Women washed what appeared to be cooking utensils at one point along its bank.

We passed by the City of the Dead, a long stretch of perhaps two miles of what looked like abandoned buildings and gravesites. Our guide told us these structures were used as burial grounds for the deceased. There were exquisite shrine-mosques and mausoleums. I was in awe of the great extent of this "city." It was explained that many people from the large homeless population took up residence there.

Our tour visited a papyrus factory, where beautiful hieroglyphic-like papyrus artwork was sold. We were told these were authentic papyrus works, to be distinguished from the less valuable banana leaf productions. I got to see what the green papyrus plant looked like growing in the wild before it was harvested to be processed. In ancient days, papyrus was used as writing paper.

The pyramids of Giza and the Sphinx were incredible. I remember standing at the foot of the largest pyramid, gazing up toward its peak, just trying to contemplate the herculean effort required to construct such a structure. At times my concentration was interrupted by the Hey Joe's who sold tickets, headwear, and other assorted wares. The Great Pyramid of King Khufu was built 4,500 years ago from over two-million 2.5-ton blocks of cut stone.

Looking out toward the west, there was nothing to be seen but the Libyan Desert. Wild dogs roamed the sun-scorched, desolate landscape. Only a few sporadic cars traversed the sandy terrain. Camels loafed or sauntered about. We were cautioned about the camel drivers, that they might not charge you much to get on a camel, but that once they got you up onto the animal there would be an additional, greater charge to get you off.

A few stores were arranged huddled together a short walking distance from the pyramids, resembling a Wild West ghost town sitting in the middle of the desert. All kinds of Aladdin's lamps, water pitchers, papyrus, hookahs, incense, woodwork, brass and copper items, and other goods were sold there.

We moved on to the Egyptian Museum, which contained more than ten-thousand ancient items including some seventeen-hundred items from the tomb of King Tutankhamen. There were reliefs, sarcophagi, papyri, funerary art, and contents of various tombs other than King Tut's. There were jewelry, ornaments, and statues. Chills ran down my spine as I observed the ancient papyrus boat designs while being very aware that my childhood hero, the Norwegian archeologist Thor Heyerdahl, had used this same museum to study and plan his famous Ra Expeditions. To be standing in the same place was too good to be true.

Our guide for the entire Cairo tour was a delightful Norwegian-Egyptian woman who carried a tall wire pole with a yellow flag at the top so our group could see where she was at all times. And when she required us to muster around her, she let out a very loud yodel. She was a humorous and colorful character, and very knowledgeable of Egyptology.

We stayed overnight at the very modern Movenpik Hotel, where we were treated to a massive outdoor buffet complete with belly-dancers and Arabic music. The average temperature this time of the year was eighty-five degrees Fahrenheit. Cairo's desert climate contrasted dry, hot days with cool nights freshened by Nile River breezes. The food included eggplant, cheese-filled pastries, shish kebab, meat finger patties, yogurt with garlic, stuffed grape leaves, and fava beans. A refreshing drink called Karkade was made from plants grown in Aswan. When darkness set in, we returned to the Gaza pyramids and were treated to a sound and light show that illuminated the landmarks.

The following day, the expedition continued with a visit to the step pyramids of Memphis/Sakkara. These were smaller and different in appearance from the Giza pyramids. The steps represented a giant stairway on which the buried kings could climb to the sky.

At another site, we entered doorways leading into the earth, reminiscent of entrances to abandoned coal mines I had explored in my Pennsylvania homeland. We went underground, exploring narrow, low-ceilinged tunnels which led to dead-end tombs. We saw hieroglyphics scrawled upon the dimly-lit walls. The tunnels were quite long. Flash photography was prohibited because of its reportedly incrementally detrimental effects on the wall art.

Later, we drove to the site where President Anwar Sadat was assassinated in 1981, which I immediately recognized from my memory of the television images of that incident. We also visited his memorial, a pyramidal arch guarded by soldiers.

We visited a rug factory. It was fascinating to watch the young girls of perhaps seven years of age weaving carpets, their tiny hands working so rapidly and efficiently. Four girls sat next to each other to construct one carpet. One of the girls kept sneaking glances that were filled with smiles at us.

At the end of the second day of the expedition, we departed Cairo to make the journey back to Alexandria and then the ship. We left behind the exotic world of pyramids, sand, pharaohs, camels, hieroglyphics, papyrus, mummies, tombs, and mosques.

Back aboard the ship, I ran in the 5K on the flight deck and got the Egypt 5K Run tee shirt. Eleven laps around the flight deck was the equivalent of five kilometers. Departing Egypt on the 4th of September, we spent the next seven or eight days underway.

Around September 11, 1988, USS Kennedy anchored at Toulon, France. Although Special Services offered tours to Paris via the Bullet Train, Monte Carlo—to see the Jacques Cousteau Museum and the world famous casino, Tignes—considered the most beautifully equipped ski resort in the world and home of the 1990 Winter Olympics, St. Tropez—situated in one of the most beautiful bays of the French Riviera, and a couple other places, most sailors chose to remain in the quiet, picturesque seaport of Toulon.

The weather was warm, perfect for sunbathing on the sandy French Riviera beaches. Of course we could not help but notice that it was the vogue for the women to sunbathe topless there. The water was beautiful, sparkling, and clean.

Toulon was a nautical city of two-hundred thousand, with the feel of a small town. It was one of the two major French naval bases in the Mediterranean, the other being Marseilles, about thirty miles away. Toulon was the homeport of the French Navy's Mediterranean Fleet. The majority of the population was connected in some way to either the navy or commercial shipbuilding.

I was struck by how quiet, peaceful, and clean this city was. Many of the sailors made phone calls to home from Toulon, using a tele-carte, which was a credit card providing a prepaid telephone call of a predetermined duration.

There was a picturesque view to be had from the top of Mont Faron, which could be reached by cable car. The panoramic view of the city and harbor was spectacular.

One day, LCDR Wallace and I took a train to Bandol, eighteen kilometers away. We had a long, relaxed dinner at an outdoor restaurant overlooking a gorgeous white sand beach.

Another day I travelled all over the city with a group from the Dental Department, checking out stores and brasseries (snack bars). The currency exchange rate was approximately six French francs to one dollar. Most people did not speak much English, so we communicated a lot by sign language and short phrases. We strode around the outdoor shopping mall, checked out the people, and had giant ice cream cones. Middle-aged women and older were in incredibly great shape, unlike in America or other places where plumpness tended to set in. We had pizza with toppings of squid and mussels.

We met a couple girls who played a mean game of foosball, beating us soundly during our friendly competition. We got even with them, however, when we triumphed at pinball. We met two French guys who were culinary students, who carried their "toolboxes" filled with a variety of cooking utensils.

At a stylish, old-fashioned tavern where a large, shiny bald-headed, handlebar-mustached gentleman tended bar, we ate dinner and partied down with some of the locals. Later in the night we moved outdoors to one of the sidewalk cafeteria tables and met two comedians who could speak a little English. We spent a few hours past midnight naming bands and their songs, attempting to perform their hits by either singing some of the lines or improvising musical instruments. One guy played "trumpet" with his lips.

Another did the guitar parts. I played bass by blowing air into the side of my palm, while someone else provided percussion on the tabletop. In addition, we may have had an air guitar demonstration or two. You could say that we bonded with the French during our stay in Toulon.

Another evening I strolled down some of the seedier parts of the town with two of the ship's civilian teachers who were part of the crew during the cruise. This particular bar district was complete with beckoning prostitutes and drunken sailors. One facility had a fabulous jukebox, so we hoisted a few beers and toasted "Viva La France!" to some of the locals. Stevie Wonder's *I just Called to Say I Love you* played and I thought of home in the States.

Several members of the ship's crew brought their bicycles along on the cruise, finding any available nook they could aboard the ship in which to secure and store them. DT3 Keith Hollenback was one of the lucky sailors who used his own bike to tour the French countryside. I tried to rent a bike but unfortunately found the place closed the day I was able to venture out to it.

On one of my duty days aboard the ship, I volunteered as an escort for visiting dignitaries. The Marines were putting on a Sunset Parade. The escorts dressed in the formal choker whites. I gave a guided tour to two beautiful French girls and a French naval officer who came with them. They kept asking to see Tom Cruise's plane, so I led them to the flight deck and showed them an F-14 aircraft. They were elated.

As the sun began to set, we went below to the hangar bay where chairs were set up. A rather large group of visitors was gathered. After everyone took their seats, one of the ship's aircraft elevators dramatically dropped from the flight deck, conveying the JFK's highly trained Silent Drill Team. Dressed handsomely in their formal uniforms, these Marines sharply slapped their rifles into different positions with precise, measured body movements. The exercise was intended to demonstrate the Corps' discipline and attention to detail.

Following the Sunset Parade was an informal reception in which wine, punch, cake, and other refreshments were served. I met an inquisitive French naval officer named Captain Delort. He was very congenial and spoke English fairly well. We talked for a while and he invited me to have dinner sometime. I got his phone number and promised to contact him after I checked my schedule for the remaining time we would be in Toulon.

The next day I went ashore and called Captain Delort's home. His wife, who spoke extremely little English, at least immediately recognized my name. Her husband had spoken to her of our expected meeting. She tried to tell me how we could rendezvous, but we could not understand each other no matter how much we tried. With much difficulty I was able to determine that he was not home and that I should call back "in fifteen minutes."

So I waited and returned the call in the designated time, but he was still not home. She was distressed. I said I would call again later.

This time, after hanging up, I spotted three young French lasses hanging out on the street corner. I went over to the girls and asked if any of them spoke English. One said "a little," as she showed me how little by displaying a distance of about an inch between her thumb and forefinger. That was good enough for me. I asked if she would help me and she excitedly agreed to do her best.

I explained that "I am trying to talk to some woman on the phone . . ." The three girls giggled and simultaneously sang out "Ohhh?" as if to say "Aha! Now tell us the rest of this juicy story!" I said, "No—not what you think. Her husband speaks English, but he is not home . . ." They loved that. Together, they let out an even bigger "Ahhh hahh?" I said, "No—not what you think!"

I explained the rest of the story as they listened attentively with big smiles and more giggles. We called and I put my volunteer on the phone to speak to Mrs. Delort. She conveyed the necessary information to my new translator friend. I found out where and when to meet the Captain and his wife for dinner. We hung up and I thanked the girls for their help.

Later, I met Monsieur Delort at our rendezvous point and we made our way to his small apartment. I met his wonderful wife, with whom I had struggled through two phone conversations, and his fourteen-year old daughter, Magali. Inside Magali's bedroom was a huge poster from the movie, *Top Gun*, which seemed to be quite the popular flick out here.

We had an excellent dinner at a restaurant overlooking the Mediterranean. Captain Delort was fascinated by the American ability to get things done, to make things happen. He said, "We French are thoughtful and smart like the Americans, but we seem not to be able to take ideas forward and make things happen as you can." We talked about Magali's love of horseback riding. Following dinner, we said goodbye and wished each other the best of luck always.

The USS Kennedy left France on September 21st. We would be at sea for the next eighteen days, which felt like a long time after having toured so many places ashore.

When at sea, one has ample opportunity to engage in interesting conversation. Everone had something to contribute. I had one discussion, for example, with DA Chris Spiridigliozzi (or "Sprig" for short), one of our dental technicians, at the port sponson. Short, with boyish face and round wire-framed glasses, he was a thoughtful young kid. He told me we lived aboard a "Death Ship," capable of inflicting great damage if called upon. He also explained, with his characteristic grin, that "Every enlisted has a sob story." In other words, generally there was something tragic that had happened to each enlisted individual's life, such as parents divorcing or some kind of failure back home. So they "joined the Navy." All they wanted was a chance to feel essential by being part of something larger like a family. In many ways, the Navy was like a family, perhaps giving them that chance. Here, they worked together and there certainly was at least some degree of camaraderie.

One day, Chief Gonzalez asked me if I wanted to see where the enlisteds were berthed. It was a long walk from Dental to their forward berthing, somewhere near the bow of the ship. I was amazed at how small an area it was that housed the enlisted personnel of Dental. They were crammed into a U-shaped corner, with sets of three bunks stacked from the deck up. A curtain could be drawn for privacy when desired, for example to take a noontime nap.

Under each rack was a storage compartment. It did not seem like the greatest of conditions but was an improvement over sailing days as late as the early 1960's when, according to one of the Kennedy's Command Master Chiefs, ABCM Sissell, "Back then, quality of life consisted of canvas racks stacked four-high, no air conditioning and water hours." He recalled that ventilation was poor and "most people slept out on the catwalks to escape the heat."

When I arrived, there were three guys reading. A couple others had their curtains drawn. Within thirty seconds, one by one about six little heads popped out from the racks, everyone happily greeting me. They were so pleased to see me visiting, showing some interest in their lives. They excitedly gave me a complete tour of their living spaces.

Flight ops were halted for a few hours, so it was announced over the 1MC that the deck was open for jogging. It felt like a perfect day to stretch out the legs and get fresh air. So I went with LT Rongone and the Chief to the flight deck. LCDR Rick Sobie, back ashore in the States at NNSY, advised me to get a good pair of running shoes for such occasions. An advanced runner, he instructed me on the exact specifications needed for the particular type of footwear best suited for my feet. "The flight deck is rough on the feet," he declared. So I bought a pair as the doctor had ordered, and they served me very well during the Cruise.

Some aircraft were below deck in the hangar, while others were atop the flight deck with wings folded. There was plenty of room to jog. We ran along the periphery, being careful not to go over the edge. The flat ocean horizon surrounded us. No land or ships were to be seen. The sun beamed down and a moderately cool breeze wafted across the open space. This was top of the world, to be able to run on this enormous vessel with nothing but water surrounding us on all sides! What a view.

Life aboard a United States aircraft carrier was like living in what was often described as a city afloat. The ship's personnel were divided into departments that made up that city.

There was the Administrative Department, responsible for the ship's newspaper, TV, radio, print shop, post office, and lawyer's office. They were the folks in charge of Special Services, which provided the tours and port information. They maintained enlisted career records and provided career counseling.

AIMD (Aircraft Intermediate Maintenance Department) provided maintenance on the aircraft. Comprised of four-hundred fifty personnel, the department was subdivided into twenty-six diverse work centers providing direct support to the air wing.

The Air Department, led by the Air Boss, CDR Larry Francisco, included all the different colored shirts discussed previously. He was featured in a film created aboard the ship that was entitled, *Air Boss.*

The Religious Ministries Department was comprised of one Catholic priest and two Protestant ministers and about six enlisted support personnel. They ran the library and chapel.

The Communications Department was composed of seventy-two radiomen and four officers. Operating around the clock and equipped with radio, computer, and satellite equipment, they exchanged rapid and secure messages with other commands throughout the world. On average, they sent, received, and processed more than two-thousand messages daily.

The Deck Department was engaged in watchstanding on the bridge, anchoring and mooring of the ship, standing anchor and deck watches to provide for the safety and security of the ship in port, painting the ship's hull, manning the motor whaleboat crew to save a man lost overboard, and providing all boating services to the crew while at anchor. They were responsible for running the underway replenishment rigs to receive the fuel and cargo necessary to keep the ship running.

The Engineering Department was responsible for the ship's heating, air conditioning, refrigeration, steam system, water pumps, 1MC sound system, electricity, lighting, sound-powered phones, fire department, locksmith services, propulsion, and desalination. In this department were the welders, pipe fitters, sheet metal workers, and plumbers.

The Marine Detachment served as the ship's security force, maintaining a high state of readiness for rapid response to terrorism and ship emergencies.

The Medical Department had six officers and about thirty corpsmen. After eating all that delicious food in Egypt, I became very ill and dehydrated and, thanks to Medical, was able to be treated at three in the morning when the going got rough. After barely staggering down all the ladders to get to Main Medical, they hooked me up with an IV and I immediately felt human again.

MMD (Maintenance Management Department) was responsible for scheduling to ensure the accomplishment of preventative maintenance on thousands of equipment components. They coordinated repairs between work centers and between the ship and private contractors. They ensured all repairs were carried out safely and expediently.

The Navigation Department ensured the safe and accurate movement of the ship.

The Operations Department mission was to collect, evaluate, and disseminate combat and operational information necessary to the assigned tasking of the ship and her aircraft. They were responsible for planning, scheduling, and coordinating all ship and air wing evolutions.

The Safety Department was tasked with carrying out safety awareness programs and monitoring shipboard evolutions for unsafe working conditions, hazards, and practices.

The Security Department was the police station of the ship, complete with its own brig.

The Supply Department maintained about forty-four storerooms containing $23.2 million worth of goods during the Med Cruise, while shipping and receiving over 19,000 pieces of cargo. The cooks and kitchen staff were part of Supply, providing not just the shipboard meals but also the food at the fleet landing barbecues. The Supply Department was also responsible for the ship's laundry, dining areas, and berthing.

The Training Department provided educational and human resource training and support.

The Weapons Department was responsible for procuring, handling, stowing, and assembling the explosives.

It seemed it was always an adventure whenever I had to go to a space on the ship in which I was unfamiliar. For example, I had to travel to the office where small electronic equipment was tested and certified to be safe to use aboard ship. First I had to climb ladders to the proper level. Next I walked through the long passageway that seemed to have no end. Then I found a way to cross to the other side of the ship. The way these passageways were laid out reminded me of Boston's confusing layout, with no organized pattern as could be found in a more modern, planned city such as Orlando, Florida.

Arriving at the other side of the ship, I read the location markings printed on the bulkhead and proceeded in the direction indicated in my written road directions. Then I discovered an "alleyway" which led me outboard. Proceeding too far, I opened a hatch onto the catwalk, exposed to the ocean. You could see huge waves crashing down below from this point. Returning inside the ship, I finally located the proper door to the electronics shop. Entering, I saw coffee mugs and small fans for ventilation—commonplace items throughout the ship. Some petty officer greeted me. This was his turf, where he spent most of his working hours aboard the ship. This was his "neighborhood," his stomping grounds of which he was most familiar. After having my radio tested and certified, I departed and began the adventurous journey back to my own neighborhood of this large shipboard city.

From October 11 to October 17, the ship anchored in the incredibly scenic crescent-shaped bay of Antalya, Turkey. A visit to a Turkish port was unusual during a Med Cruise, but we were fortunate to have been given this opportunity. Not knowing what to expect ashore, we disembarked and discovered a pleasant surprise.

The calm bay waters offered a short boat ride to fleet landing. With the towering snow-capped Taurus Mountains as a backdrop, this was perhaps the most scenic anchorage during the deployment. And the Turks were wonderfully friendly and gracious hosts.

Due to its spectacular colors, the stretch of the southern Turkish coastline from Fethiye to Alanya was referred to as the Turquoise

Coast. The magnificent beaches were supposed to have been a favorite place frequented by Cleopatra, the Queen of Egypt. The seascape was filled with secluded coves, bays, creeks, and tiny islands. Rocky crags and caves eroded by the wind and water penetrated into the coastline. Emerald green pines grew to the water's edge in many places. The turquoise sea reflected the lush vegetation of palm trees, oleanders, and lemon trees.

Antalya was the principle resort of the Turkish Riviera, bathed in sunshine for three-hundred days a year. The Germans, we were told, had recently discovered this charming place, preferring it to the crowded beaches elsewhere in Europe.

Once ashore, we encountered shoe shine kids who would leap out and put a smudge of shoe polish on your footwear in hopes that you would then pay them to finish the job. There was also a cute little child who approached us with hopes that we would buy a flower from her. I wondered what her parents were like and if she went to school. Did she have any brothers and sisters? A young boy approached me with a box of Bazooka Joe bubble gum, the kind with the folded comic strip inside the outside wrapper. The comic strip jokes were printed in Turkish. He did not speak English so I asked him as best I could how much three pieces of gum cost. I gave him the money and he proceeded to give me the whole box, but I waved him off and took only three individual pieces of gum. He looked astonished as I handed the box back to him. At the price he quoted me, to take the whole box would have been a steal.

An estimated fifty-million people (1984 census) occupied Turkey, a country slightly larger than Texas. The principal language was Turkish, which was related to Finnish and Hungarian.

A long flight of wide stone steps took us from fleet landing up the cliff into the city. Shady, palm-lined boulevards traversed through the business district. There was a great variety of places in which to shop, ranging from modern shops and boutiques to colorful bazaars and bustling markets. In these places you could find harem rings, intricately patterned carpets, brass, beaten copper vessels, hand-painted plates of kutahya, items of onyx and meerschaum, leather jackets, and jewelry such as bracelets adorned with precious and semiprecious stones. Somewhere out there I bought a little "Aladdin's lamp." I also obtained two cassettes of Turkish music. One of these, by singer Zerrin Ozer, would prove to be a favorite of mine even years later.

Bread was baked fresh daily. Lamb, rice, or yogurt were basic ingredients of many of the dishes. When whisked with cold water, the yogurt formed ayran, a refreshing popular drink. Turkish coffee, a thick brew, was available. Breakfast was light: tea, white cheese, olives, and bread with butter, jam or honey. The largest meal was dinner, typically served in the late evening. Eggplant was the premier vegetable, used to prepare, for example, hunkarbegendi, a puree with casseroled lamb. Borek was flaky pastry pies stuffed with meat or cheese. And for desert there was baklava, but also many other delicious sweets. In summer, many Turks preferred to end their meals with grapes, peaches, apricots, figs, and melons grown in the countryside. The national drink was the licorice-flavored liqueur, raki.

I spent two days taking organized tours of the surrounding area. In Perge, we rummaged through toppled columns and stone slabs strewn over the ground, the ruined remnants of Roman civilization. In Aspendos, we sat in the stone bleachers of a well-preserved ancient theatre that was still standing and actually used for presentation of plays in current times. Its thirty-nine flights of steps could seat almost twenty-thousand spectators. In Side, there was another Roman theatre and beautiful waterfront.

We explored a most exotic forested park which had dirt paths and rock slabs to walk upon. In places, there were stepping stones on which to cross over streams while gazing at the scenic landscape. There were crooked rock staircases to follow while you twisted and maneuvered through dense vegetation that wrapped itself around the thoroughfare, creating a sort of floral tunnel. There were misshapen tree trunks under which to duck. Every turn in the path led to a uniquely different situation upon the navigable terrain.

The first tour guide spoke English very well and frequently sang lines from Joe Cocker songs. He wore a USS Kennedy ball cap and sunglasses secured by a cord around his neck. A proponent of Turkey's Westernization, he proudly told of his hero, the Turk leader Ataturk, and his reforms. But he also sounded cautious when he spoke of the threat to modernization from fundamentalist forces who were gaining strength in steering the nation away from the West.

I took a swim in the Turquoise Coast waters. It was difficult to walk in the water because the floor was composed of six-inch rounded rocks and smaller pebbles that were hazardous to the feet. The water temperature was warm and the scenic view of the shoreline from out in the water was spectacular.

The second tour guide walked with a limp which resulted, if my memory serves me well, from a fall off a horse in his younger days. His English was a little more difficult to understand than the other guide's. He told tales of the countryside where he grew up. About half of the nation's population resided in agricultural villages.

In addition to the organized tours, I explored Antalya on my own. Walking down the main boulevard, I arrived at a park where I sat at the precipice of a cliff overlooking the bay. I gazed in wonder for a considerable time at a most remarkable view of the USS Kennedy anchored in the clear blue waters, the magnificent Taurus Mountains serving as a backdrop. Pines lined the cliff. The mountains seemed painted in varying shades of grey, the effect of shadowing as the sun gradually set, creating a spectacular visual effect on the individual mountain peaks that seemed compressed together. The park surroundings were peaceful and serene. For a few minutes, the prayer of a muezzin could be heard emanating from a nearby mosque.

On the way back to the ship, I paused at the scenic overlook high above fleet landing. From this promontory I could see the brown, wooden rooftops of many homes, presenting the appearance of thatch. Several mosques decorated the landscape, with one fluted minaret standing out.

I met a friendly Turk, about my age, who offered to take me to a place where I could get good photos. We took a "bus," which was actually a rather large public transportation van filled to the brim with passengers of all ages, about three miles down along the coast.

We got off adjacent to a cliffside park filled with beautiful views of the Mediterranean Sea. Communication was difficult, as my friend did not speak very much English, but not impossible as we groped through various conversations. After we had completed a tour of the surroundings, he guided me back to fleet landing.

On a fourth day, I went to the USS Kennedy's private beach club, where food and drinks were served. There were about twenty people from the ship sitting at outdoor tables when an old, well-weathered, hunched-over man with several missing front teeth came by with a tank hooked up to his back. He whipped out a hose and began squirting what smelled like bug spray at the tables. I guessed it was just the designated time of the day to spray for insects at the club—no matter that there were people around. He thought nothing about the large clouds of spray that floated around our heads. A few of us thought the sight was hilarious and we dove for cover beneath the tables, pretending we were getting attacked by mortar fire. When he saw us carrying on, he flashed a toothless grin that made all of us on the ground laugh even harder. Then he simply returned to the job at hand, thinking nothing of spraying more clouds of toxic chemicals our way, periodically flashing another grin, with an expression on his face indicating he couldn't figure out why we were acting so strangely. We evacuated the area, figuring he had no clue about OSHA-like regulations.

The USS Kennedy departed Antalya on the 17th of October. In four days we would anchor near Tunis, Tunisia on the continent of Africa.

The boat ride to fleet landing in Tunisia was about fifty minutes long in rough seas. We saw small grey warships called corvettes as we approached the shore. Many individuals got seasick.

Tunisia was the smallest country in the region. It was bordered on the west and southwest by Algeria, and Libya to its southeast. The rest of the nation bordered the Mediterranean Sea, offering a seven-hundred fifty mile coastline. About eight and a half million people lived there.

The desert climate of southern Tunisia, with frequent siroccos (hot southerly winds) blowing in from the Sahara Desert, was characterized by much higher daytime temperatures than in the north.

Tunisia's population was largely a mixture of Arab and Berber. The Berbers settled there first, and then the Arabs came to the area in the 7th century A.D. The majority of the people were Muslim.

Tunisia's official language was Arabic, although French was widely spoken. In the late 1800's, Tunisia was caught between French, British, and Italian aspirations. In a deal consummated in 1881, the French acquired Tunisia solely for themselves as a protectorate. In 1956, France granted full independence to the land.

We were well aware that the Palestine Liberation Organization (PLO) had its headquarters in Tunis, having relocated after it was forced to leave Beirut, Lebanon in 1982.

Just a year before our port visit, in 1987, Habib Bourguiba, a Tunisian leader who took the nation into a Western orientation, left his position of power. Together with the rise of Islamic fundamentalism and increased ties to the Arab world, his departure had produced a very different atmosphere in the nation.

It was into this uncertain land that we were cast as visitors. Leaving fleet landing, a group of us from the carrier climbed into a bus and were driven past dozens of pink flamingos as we passed through the city of Tunis, eventually arriving at the Old City of Medina, where we entered a long tunnel which housed a marketplace called the Souk. Each side of the tunnel was lined with shops. The air smelled like an old tavern. Merchants eagerly awaited our business.

Like in Egypt, the art of bargaining was the expected means to purchase goods. The ship's Catholic chaplain, Father Kurilec, wished to buy a tin tea set, so he began negotiations with a vendor. The markup in price, we discovered, for everything there was incredibly high; but the vendors, after a bout of bargaining, would greatly lower the cost. Father Kurilec was not satisfied enough, however, when the vendor sliced the price tag a few times; he wanted to go that extra mile. So they haggled some more. I watched with fascination as the process played out. By now the vendor was sweating and excused himself to check with his boss for permission to lower the price still more. He returned in a few minutes and accepted the lower bid, and the sale was closed.

By this time I had grown fond of the tea set myself. So I told the salesman that I would buy one also—but at the same price the preceding customer had gotten it for. The look on his face turned from enthusiastic to one of total defeat as he shook his head, claiming he could not do it. I said I would not want it then. He reconsidered and said, "For the same price as him?" as he pointed to the priest. I nodded. He reluctantly sold me the tea set for that same price. It was not a bad deal for me—the chaplain did all the dirty work and I just rode in on the tide afterwards.

Our tour guide took us to a carpet shop. We were given seats along the walls of a large room. Green-colored mint tea was served. A salesman entered and spoke about the high quality of his rugs. He summoned his aide, who began unrolling a variety of beautifully-designed rugs. The aide labored hard, sweating profusely in the process as he struggled to lift up the heavy rugs for display to his audience. I don't know if any of the Navy people bought any rugs that day.

We toured the ruins of the ancient city of Carthage, founded on the north coast of Africa in 814 B.C. by the Phoenicians. Being at this site was a very special moment to me because I remembered vividly as a child having studied all about the Carthaginians. From the middle of the third century to the middle of the second century B.C., Carthage was engaged in the Punic Wars with Rome. These clashes ended in the complete defeat of Carthage in 146 B.C. when this site was plundered and burned. We climbed around the remnants of this once great city: stone slabs, rocks, and columns of various sizes, some standing but most laying collapsed and strewn about this raised elevation overlooking the deep blue waters of the Mediterranean Sea.

After eating lunch at Sidi Boussaid, a resort overlooking the Med, we drove to our last destination, the Bardo Museum, which was famous for its collection of Roman mosaics, which were gorgeous. Mosaics were surface decorations created by inlaying small pieces of variously colored materials to form pictures or patterns. Mosaics were everywhere in the museum—on the ceilings, on the walls, and on many functional and decorative objects.

Departing Tunis on the 24th of October, we were at sea for about the next four days. On October 28, 1988 the ship anchored in Palma, Spain. This port was on the island of Majorca, one of the Balearic Islands, off the eastern coast of mainland Spain.

It was interesting to visit Spain, the land from which came the first European settlers to establish a permanent presence in the Americas. Spain was the first European country in modern times to possess a large overseas empire, spurred on in that endeavor by its nautical prowess. Fearless, seagoing explorers and its once-powerful navy allowed the growth of such a large empire.

The Balearic Islands were occupied at different times by Carthaginians, Byzantines, Moslems, Romans, and even pirates. Majorca contained two mountainous regions occupying the eastern and western thirds of the island, separated by a lowland. The island's varied landscapes included pine forests, olive groves, steep gullies, and intensely terraced slopes and fertile valleys. One day I was driven through this scenic topography to a place where I went horseback riding, taking in the Spanish countryside.

One evening, I went with a large group from the ship to the Castell Comte Mal, a tourist attraction that imitated a medieval castle, complete with a banquet feast of whole chicken, wine, pizza, potatoes, peanuts, and soup. Food was served on tin, and diners were to eat with fingers only and no utensils. Upon entering the castle, we were greeted by the king and queen. We then took our seats in the bleachers around a jousting field. Each section of the audience rooted for a particular knight. My section was for the Red Knight. The jousting began. It was a fight to the death with swords and lances. A black midget dressed in a jester's outfit went around to each section, egging the audience on to cheer louder for its designated warrior. In the end, the Red Knight won. The place was hysterical. It was like attending American All-Star Wrestling. It was crazy fun, a good release for the ship's crew.

One evening, the Dental Department held its own dinner at a Palma restaurant. Enroute to the restaurant, Steve Wallace and I took a few wrong turns and found ourselves walking through old, narrow medieval streets. The buildings were mostly residential and were veneered with stucco. The streets were cobblestone. We felt as if we had gone back in time.

At last arriving at the restaurant, we joined the rest of the dental crew and sampled the Spanish cuisine. There was paella, which was yellow rice mixed with a variety of seafood such as lobster, shrimp, mussels, and scallops. There were tapas, an appetizer. I had the roast suckling pig, which was very good and tender.

The Cathedral, also called the Seo, was the dominant landmark of Palma. This graceful gothic cathedral was impressive. Its formidable, upward-reaching lines towered above. Its construction began in the year 1230 A.D. and was not completed until 1601. Made from golden limestone, the cathedral was one-hundred twenty-one meters long and fifty-five meters wide, with a double row of flying arches. It overlooked the verdant Plaza de la Reina.

Via Roma was the street known for its central tree-lined sidewalk bordered by rows of newspaper stands and flower stalls. Ornate lampposts stood tall, embellishing the popular hangout.

Somewhere in the shopping area I met a woman named Liane who had fled from her residence in South Africa because of her political views. She opposed the system of apartheid that existed there. Coming to Palma, she opened a store that sold African wares. I bought two hand-carved wooden decorative masks and a sculpture of a male tribal figure holding a stick, all imported from central Africa.

The officers of the Medical and Dental Departments got together to hold an *admin* during the port call in Palma. An admin was a rendezvous point in a liberty port, a place to party, sleep, and stage social operations. This idea was said to have been started by pilots years ago. The first day of the admin, I went ashore with LT John Biddulph, a physician and New Jersey native. We bought the food and drinks to stock up the rented hotel rooms of the admin. After transporting the goods to the rooms, we went topside to the roof of the hotel to lie out in the sun. The hotel had modern accommodations and allowed excellent panoramic views of the surrounding area. I listened to Spanish radio stations through my Sony Walkman, picking up music like that of Julio Iglesias. It was warm outside, a beautiful day.

In the evening, besides greeting others from the ship who visited the admin, John and I took a cab to the nearby resort of Magalluf. Some of the best nightclubs we experienced during the Med Cruise were there.

On another night, after returning to the ship, intending to call it a night, I realized I forgot my stateroom key back at the admin hotel. It was about two or three in the morning. Rather than cause a commotion waking everyone up trying to find a spare key, I got back on the boat to return to shore. The clubs in Spain stayed open very late so I stopped in at a couple, eventually ending up at the admin, where I crashed for the night.

Special Services offered great excursions in Palma. There was a trip to La Calobra that involved a wild, scenic trek down a winding mountain road, descending to a tunnel and beach. There was a visit to the secluded Lluch Monastery to see the famous statue of the Black Virgin, often called "La Morenita" because of the dark coloration the wood had assumed over time. There was an excursion to the Caves of Drach, one of the largest underground lakes in the world. The existence of this cave was well-known in ancient times, but no one ever was adventurous enough to explore it. But in 1878 three people got lost inside and found their way back to the surface thirty hours later after having wandered aimlessly through it wondering if they would ever come out alive. Another excursion was to a factory specializing in the creation of man-made pearls, the most sought-after in the world, made from a central glass nucleus.

Somewhere in Mallorca I bought an ornate Spanish dagger to remind me of the conquistador's empire. Later I gave it to one of my brothers back home.

We departed Palma on November 4th and headed to Augusta, Sicily, where we anchored from the 7th to the 12th of November. This harbor was not a port of call, however; we could not leave the ship. Only personnel with a specific mission at the seaport could go ashore. To celebrate Veteran's Day, the crew held a *steel beach picnic*, in which food and drinks were served atop the flight deck.

After leaving Sicily, we returned to Naples from the 14th to the 21st of November. During this time, I took a train through the Italian countryside to Rome, along with a small group of officers from different departments of the ship. Rome was a city filled with monuments, art, interesting architecture, ancient history of a great civilization, and lively cosmopolitan life. Our group ran into Paul Teller, a civilian teacher aboard Kennedy for the cruise, who had once lived in Rome for at least a year. He took us to many of the essential landmarks such as the Spanish Steps, Coliseum, Roman Forum, and Altare della Patria. We nicknamed Paul, "Flash," because of the gruelingly swift pace he established in getting us to see all that we could see in the limited time we had available. He also made a few wrong turns as he was trying to remember where everything was located, and so there were times we would be rushing down some alleyway only to stop abruptly to turn around and try to correct course. But, darting to and fro like this, we managed to cover a lot of territory. We tossed coins into the Trevi Fountain. Legend had it that this action assured a happy return to Rome one day. We visited the Basilica of Saint Peter, climbing to the top to take in the magnificent view of the city and Tiber River. Some shipmates attended a mass celebrated by Pope John Paul II.

After we returned to the ship from Rome, I went to Pompeii, the ancient city lost to the world for a time after it was buried under the ash and lava of the volcano, Mount Vesuvius. When we began walking the grounds, we could not help but observe that here lay yet another "pile of rocks," as we described it, representing what physically remained of the ancient Roman civilization. Attesting to their widespread influence was the fact that we had seen their stone and concrete rubble throughout the Mediterranean. Many of these fields of rocks did not look like much. However, as we continued through Pompeii, we came upon whole city block areas that were extensively excavated and were remarkably well-preserved and, as I walked through its resurrected streets, using a little imagination I could almost picture what it would have been like when the city was alive with its men, women, and children.

On another day, I experienced the cliffs of Amalfi. The twenty-six mile long winding cliffside drive along the coast of Amalfi, lying between Vietri sul Mare and Positano, was a breathtaking and magical experience. It was as if I had been transported to another world. It was unreal, with every sharp bend in the narrow road offering a different spectacular view, unrivaled by anything I had ever seen before. The intense blue sea and sky served as backdrop for the variously angled views of the cliffside hamlets cut from the precipice and the tiny enchanting beaches. The picturesque houses and cottages were somehow tightly arranged amidst the terraced patches of land and thick vegetation.

On the way back from the Amalfi Drive, we happened upon the city of Sorrento. *Come Back to Sorrento* was an Italian song I had long known. So here was the city for which that song was named. We toured a store where I bought a beautiful inlaid wood village scene, and then strolled briefly around the town.

There was nothing like spending an entire day in a foreign port, exploring and meeting people, and then getting a hot, grilled burger or hot dog and an ice-cold Coke at fleet landing before boarding the liberty boat back to the ship. This was a great service provided by the ship. It was a nice opportunity to meet up with other Kennedy sailors to exchange tales of our adventures. Years later, I still say these food fests at fleet landings were among the best memories of the deployment. Like the saying goes, "It just doesn't get much better than this!"

We left Naples on the 18th of November. On the way to our next port, the ship was caught in a severe storm. Doors and hatches and all weather decks were secured. I spent a few hours in my rack, feeling the ship move in a more agitated manner than usual. We encountered high 60-knot winds and heavy seas. No one was allowed on the flight deck without the permission of the Captain. Some of our planes were redirected to land at an airport on the mainland. The waves were so big that they were even crashing over the ship's bow, which was about sixty feet above the water.

On November 23rd we pulled up pierside in Marseilles, France, the second largest city in France. It was nice not to have to deal with the hassles of liberty boats. Here, since the water was sufficiently deep along the pier, we could tie up and just walk off the ship directly onto the pier.

Marseilles experienced rapid industrial growth after World War II. Despite the loss of much of its quaintness, the heart of its historic center, the Old Port, was still reminiscent of the colorful past when fishermen pulled up their boats to sell their daily catches. The Old Port was an oval inlet lined by colorful fishing boats and yachts.

Marseilles was a big city with plenty of street life. A carousel revolved on one street corner as a group of parents watched their children ride the horses. The buildings throughout the downtown were fabulous architectural structures with all kinds of nooks and ornate designs for the eye to explore.

The people of France welcomed the USS Kennedy with open arms, in part because they seemed to hold an immense fondness for the late U.S. president, who spent much time on the French Riviera and whose wife had a French background. A pleasant promenade, the President J.F. Kennedy Coastal Road, wound for a great distance along the Marseilles coastline, eventually unfolding into the center of the downtown.

As I stood in a rather long line at a McDonald's, I just happened to meet an American dentist and her husband who were living in Marseilles for a few months before they were to move to Zaire. Steve was a missionary and his wife, Sue, was to accompany him to work among the inhabitants of that central African nation. I talked a little dentistry with Sue and learned some things about French dentistry, how it differed from the American brand. After we consumed our Big Macs and fries, the friendly couple took me for a tour of the city. We passed through the transvestite section of town. We strode down the Canebiere, the most famous street in the heart of Marseilles. We saw many fascinating monuments. On a hill overlooking the Old Port was the distinguished Basilica of Notre Dame de la Garde, dating from the 8th Century A.D. Our final mission of the day was to sample the famous bouillabaisse (pronounced "boo yu bas," with the accent on either the first or last syllable), the local highly-seasoned fish soup, containing at least two types of fish. We settled on a restaurant in the Old Port and were treated to this elegant dish. It seemed a little too fishy for our tastes, however, but was worth trying out.

There was much activity on the pier to which our ship was moored. We held the PRT there. And Doc Wallace was tasked to be in charge of selling "beer on the pier" and JFK souvenirs there, the profits going to defray the costs of the cruisebook, which he was also in charge of. He sold all 320 cases of Bud, Michelob, and Miller Lite. Several of our dental technicians assisted him in these endeavors.

It was during our port call in Marseilles that one of the ship's petty officers was electrocuted while attempting to repair something in the kitchen. Sadly, all efforts at resuscitation failed. Dr. Wallace was notified that the official protocol necessitated a dental forensic exam for identification purposes, even though this was not that crucial a step in this particular situation. Antemortem records, in this case, were easy to obtain, since he was a shipmate and dental records of each crewmember were stored aboard the ship. Dr. Wallace and I performed separate postmortem exams and our results were in concurrence. It was difficult to perform the exam because the deceased's jaw would only open so wide due to the rigor mortis. It was sad to see such a previously healthy and strong young man perish as he did just trying to help his shipmates fix an electrical problem.

Some of the other sailors spent a day learning about the French Foreign Legion at the famous museum in Aubagne. Others took the Bullet Train and spent two days in Paris. There was also a tour to Avignon which included a wine-tasting opportunity.

We departed Marseilles on the 28th of November and would be at sea until mid-December.

Jogging in the hangar bay was difficult and dangerous because of all the obstacles and ongoing maintenance activity, but was permitted as long as people were careful. You had to be constantly on the watch for people and vehicles, which had a tendency to appear suddenly as you ran along. There were knee-high chains securing aircraft to the deck, eye-level airplane wings to duck under, small vehicles maneuvering about, and other hindrances to a relaxed jog. It was safer and more scenic to do pushups and situps near the elevators that were directly exposed to the ocean.

Mass Casualty drills were held periodically in the evenings. All medical personnel were involved. My job was to rush to the mess decks where I would join several others in removing salt and pepper shakers, napkin dispensers, and anything else on the long dining tables, after which we rearranged the furniture so casualties could be transferred to the tabletops for triage and treatment.

One night, as most of the crew was sleeping, we were awakened by the piercing cries of "Man Overboard!!" People crawled out of their racks, half asleep, from all corners of the ship and walked in orderly fashion, long lines moving along the passageways in the same prescribed way as during general quarters. Some were in pajamas, others in sweats. Many were barely awake, staggering like zombies. Someone on the flight deck or catwalk apparently saw a light wand fall overboard into the black sea. We could not take any chances that it may have only been the wand that fell and so Man Overboard was called. In the end, everyone assigned to the ship was accounted for. The rescue squad was recalled. These false alarms were to occur a few times during the deployment, which led the crew to believe someone was playing a stupid joke. Fortunately, it eventually ceased altogether.

Another night, we were awakened by an incident that was not a drill—a main space fuel oil leak. This was a grave situation because of the potential for the highly flammable liquid to accidentally ignite. The surrounding areas on the second and third decks were evacuated. We had to muster in the hangar bay. While we waited, at least there were some interesting views as we looked out into the dark night. Mostly all you could see were periodic glimpses of flashing lights from ocean-going vessels far away on the horizon, but also the waves nearest our own warship were illuminated slightly by the night lights of the Kennedy as she cut through the water in her forward motion. Fortunately, the situation with the fuel spill was corrected after a couple hours and we were able to return to our staterooms.

I learned from the medical staff that a few crewmembers had contemplated suicide at some point during the deployment. They were evaluated and flown off the carrier back to the States. It was said the Navy lost about sixty-five of its own each year to suicide deaths, many of the victims under twenty-five years of age. Incidents were highest during December through February. We were reminded to be alert for changes in behavior that could signal serious personal emotional problems.

When you deploy, you miss happenings back in the homeland. While we were away on this Med Cruise, George Bush Sr. was elected to become the successor to Ronald Reagan as President. Within just a few days of his election victory, he began naming his cabinet appointees, among them James Baker for Secretary of State. The United States was making claims that Libya was manufacturing chemical weapons. The football season was in full swing.

Back in the Dental Department, everyone was working hard taking care of the crew. Some stats for the months of August and September 1988: The lab technicians, DT1 Pellet and DT2 Gordon, fabricated 44 different dentures and made many denture repairs. The prophy techs, DN Lohmann and DT3 Ramos performed 455 oral prophylaxes. DN Quick zapped 1,593 x-rays.

LCDR Primley flew back to the States for two weeks to take and pass his board exam in oral and maxillofacial surgery. He missed the stay in Egypt because of this, and his assistant, DT3 Weaver Williams, looked lost without him, as he was utilized as a floater assistant during Dr. Primley's absence.

But when LCDR Primley returned, their work was cut out for them. They became very busy in the oral surgery room, where they wore colorful headbands while performing surgery. Sometime around the Antalya visit, AN Buchanan got punched by his division mate. The oral surgery team had to perform major surgery to put his badly broken jaw back together. Buchanan stayed around for a few weeks working in Dental doing administrative tasks while his jaw healed.

But after AN Buchanan was able to leave with a well-healed mandible, we took on another customer: CPL Jim Desario, who was playing football during the Marine's Birthday Picnic at Carney Park, was hit in the head by another player. His jaw was fractured. Doc Primley wired him up. CPL Desario also stayed with us in admin. We had to obtain a blender on the ship to grind food so these guys could eat since it was difficult for them to suck food through any gaps between the wired-together teeth.

Then, during the second trip to Palma, two more sailors from the USS Kennedy Battle Group, in separate incidents, fractured their jaws while engaged in fist fights. One sailor was from the USS Biddle and the other from the Kennedy. Both were brought to the Kennedy's Dental Department to get their jaws stabilized, and work in the admin department. All these guys were a big help in running Dental. It was an experience listening to them trying to talk as they hung out in the admin space. If you put your upper and lower teeth together and don't separate them, and then try to talk, you'll see what I mean.

During the last couple months of the Med Cruise, I worked with DN Rick Tubalado, originally from the Philippines, as my assistant. He had been the "night janitor" for Dental previously throughout the deployment, working 9:00 PM to 9:00 AM taking care of the second deck passageway adjacent to our department. He made sure that the critical stretch of Main Street shined for all to see as people hustled to and fro. He also cleaned the head assigned to us. He excelled as our janitor. As my assistant, he also did an outstanding job, following in Jeff Denter's footsteps as the next Sailor of the Quarter.

One of the ship's divers came to me while we were underway and said, "I was having some discomfort in this tooth, sir, and my Division Officer wanted it checked to rule out tooth squeeze." "What's that?" I asked, and then learned something new about dentistry. "Tooth squeeze," or barodontalgia, was a condition in which a tooth elicited discomfort when someone with caries, fractured teeth, or defective restorations was surrounded by increased environmental pressures, such as that experienced by divers at greater depths of the ocean. The key was to be extra meticulous to ensure divers had none of those dental conditions so they could do their jobs without hindrance from tooth pain.

Another day as I was doing an exam on a nineteen-year-old, he seriously inquired if it would be possible for me to make his canine teeth longer, "like vampire teeth." At first I thought he was jesting, but after I had my chuckle and turned my head back toward him, observing his solemn countenance, I realized he was dead serious. He explained further that he wondered if a "cap" or some kind of bonded material could be installed so he could look more like Dracula. The look on my own face changed to a sober one. I said, sympathetically, "Sorry. Can't do it. Too many people around here need cavities taken care of. We have to give them priority. It'd be another story if the Captain authorized it for a situation where, say, the military needed a vampire in some Special Ops mission. But otherwise, taxpayers wouldn't appreciate me performing this service." He seemed to understand, and left the room and said, with a distinct Lugosi accent, "Oh vell, at least I tried."

The Marines held regular security drills so they could stay on top of their skills, which might be needed at any time. When they practiced, they did so with more vigor than other military people, as if it was the real thing, and anyone that happened upon the site of their proceedings had better follow their orders. One of the dental officers brought his wife aboard one day when we were back in Norfolk. As they walked down a passageway, a large muscular Marine yelled to the couple to halt. The dentist, aware of the seriousness and ferocity with which the Corps did its job, stopped dead in his tracks. His wife, however, continued strolling ahead and, when the Marine stuck his rifle out, she said something like, "What's your problem?" and then turned to see her husband standing at attention a few paces behind, pleading with her to listen to the guy.

One day during the Med Cruise, my scheduled patient did not show up for his appointment. I waited ten minutes, checking with the front desk periodically. After documenting in his chart that he failed to show up, he eventually appeared, visibly shaken and perspiring. "What happened to you?" I asked. "Sir, I'm sorry I'm late, but I was on my way here when a bunch of Marines came flying around the corner. They started yelling at me to stop. A couple other guys had to stop, too. We must have been standing there for fifteen minutes, and I really had to whizz so I tried to sneak away. But one of them caught me and chained my arms to the railing. Finally, they finished their games and let me go." I asked him if he went to the bathroom yet. He said, "No, sir. I wanted to let you know first that I had intended to come to my appointment." I told him to go do what he had to do, and then return and we'd get his teeth taken care of.

While aboard the ship, there was a relatively high incidence of chewing tobacco use, which caused changes to occur in the soft tissues inside the lower lip, the characteristic whitish, ribbed appearance. The standard protocol was to inform the patients of the etiology and risks, namely cancer, and for them to return to the clinic if changes in color, size, shape, or texture appeared. Users of chew often carried around empty soda cans into which they would spit the juices. It became evident to me that it was most important that you ensured the can you lifted to your lips to drink from was indeed your own personal container of soda and not a coworker's chew receptacle. I saw negligence in vigilance regarding this theme once, with a rather awkward consequence. Very funny, though, to all the bystanders.

A twenty-year old guy came to me because he was bruxing (grinding) his teeth together while he slept. He just about pleaded with me asking if there was anything he could do. He bruxed so forcefully and for such extended durations at night during sleeping hours that his shipmates claimed he was "loud and obnoxious," keeping everybody awake when they needed rest. He was afraid they were going to do something crazy to him if he continued this habit, eventually pushing them to their boiling point limit. We solved the problem by making an impression of his upper teeth, upon which our lab technicians fabricated an acrylic mouthguard. He began wearing this device at night and it absorbed the occlusal forces and prevented his teeth from rubbing against each other. The noises ceased and his shipmates were able to sleep soundly again.

One of the dental techs confided in me that he had a flareup of hemorrhoids and asked if I could prescribe something that had worked in the past. He gave me the name of the medicament. I asked him "Why don't you just go through Medical?" to which he responded "Too much of a runaround." So I wrote the prescription. When the Senior Medical Officer saw the prescription during a QA check, he decided to address me. In the wardroom one eve he asked, "So do you find you get a high success rate when your hemorrhoid patients use that particular crème?" I immediately got the point he was getting at—prescribe only for conditions within your field. I got the message. When I saw the dental tech for which I had prescribed the tube of cream, I told him "Sorry. Can't prescribe any more of that stuff. Too much of a pain in the ass."

Don Primley, Mark Rongone and DT3 Keith Hollenback were CPR instructors for the ship. They taught at least five-hundred shipmates during the months of August and September.

The three dentists I worked with during the deployment were extremely talented and I truly would have felt comfortable referring any of my patients to either of them for treatment since I was confident they would do a great job. In addition, their writing in the charts was highly legible, which was a plus when working in a group practice setting, helping to facilitate communication greatly.

DN Tim Abel ("TJ") was preparing to leave the ship in January, destined for "CIVLANT" (civilian life) back in his homeland, the northwest corner of the United States. He said he had "done his time" and now was thinking about going into carpentry.

As the cruise dragged on, some of the crew became a bit homesick. DN Denter was lonely for his wife and two children, but he hung in there all right. He was receiving mail just about every day. I tried to talk to him when he got too down and he seemed to pick up. One officer was swapping dirty letters with his wife. Doctor Wallace was craving for his kids. One of the dental techs was getting all kinds of letters from some Italian girl he met in Naples. She wrote, "I love you even though we just met!"

DT3 Paul Huff had recently arrived aboard the ship. New arrivals were given the important task of "mail buoy watch," which was actually a big joke. Fledgling personnel reporting to the ship were sufficiently briefed as to how the mail arrived aboard the ship: it would be floating on the surface of the ocean in several large buoyant bags. Personnel assigned to mail buoy watch would have to don their general quarters gear and remain at the ready on a weather deck close to the surface of the water, keeping an eye out for the mail as it floated by. At just the right moment they would use long poles to snag it and lift it out of the water. They were reminded that the entire crew was depending upon their vigilance and skill in accomplishing the mission. DT3 Huff performed exceedingly well, paving the way for his sustained outstanding performance into the future. He did so well that the chief may have sent him on another mission, to search throughout the ship for a "right-handed smoke shifter."

Sometime in 1988, there was an incident of medical waste washing up on North Carolina beaches. It was traced to the USS Coral Sea, another aircraft carrier. A message was generated from CINCLANTFLT providing interim guidance concerning new rules for the disposal of medical waste at sea, pending more definitive policies.

The message stated that medical waste was to be divided into two categories: that which was potentially infectious and that which was not. Potentially infectious waste (PIW) was deemed "waste which may contain pathogens with sufficient virulence and quantity so that exposure to the waste by a susceptible host could result in an infectious disease." Included as PIW were "sharps," any objects representing the potential for wounding and cross-contamination of persons who might someday be exposed to those sharp items. For example, these might pierce through a heavy plastic trash bag and injure the garbage man. Blood-soaked gauze was also classified as PIW.

We were directed to sterilize all PIW and then store it aboard ship until which time it could be incinerated or disposed of in port at appropriate dumping sites. Overboard discharge would be authorized only if retention of PIW would endanger the health or safety of the crew, create an unacceptable nuisance, or compromise combat readiness, provided the discharge was carried out under explicit conditions: when greater than fifty miles from a shore and only after the waste was properly packaged and weighted for negative buoyancy. Whenever we dumped overboard, we would place several of the small bags into one large bag, along with heavy objects such as the scrap metal parts we obtained from the flight deck so that the bags would sink. In actuality, though, very little hazardous waste was ever dumped overboard. Shore disposal in foreign ports was the most common method of waste removal from the ship during this deployment. The ship probably paid more to have medical wastes disposed in those ports, and one had to wonder if the rough-looking foreign waste-handlers just didn't dump the medical waste in the same place as the rest of the trash.

Previous to this message, *all* trash originating from the ship's medical spaces was simply bagged and dumped over the fantail without first being sterilized in an autoclave. All garbage originating from elsewhere on the ship was also thrown overboard as well. It was an amazing sight the first time I saw a long trail of perhaps forty bags of trash tossed over the stern, floating behind in the ship's wake. It was said that the Soviet ships used to wait until American ships had moved away from the bags, at which time they would scoop them up to rifle through and analyze the contents for anything that might assist their spy program.

When the message came out, I was appointed the department's Hazardous Waste Officer. I wrote a common sense plan following the spirit of the message, but with all the anxiety that arose from the Coral Sea crisis the plan got altered by higher authority aboard the ship: *all* waste originating from any of the dental spaces was to be considered PIW and required autoclaving. We were autoclaving candy wrappers and even coffee grounds, and other things which were obviously not infectious. Since we only had access to a small autoclave of perhaps ten inches in width, we had to package the wastes into small, log-shaped rolls so they would fit into the autoclave. We spent the good part of each day sterilizing the trash, after which we would store it in the tiny, musty closet adjacent to the waiting room. The workhorse autoclave was going full blast almost constantly.

In the beginning, we had insufficient storage space for the waste, but eventually were able to store some of the waste in the Medical Department. About 192 bags were packaged for the autoclave in December of 1988, and about 129 in January of the next year. I had to ensure that each trash bag was appropriately identifiable as "Biohazardous" and labeled with the corresponding logbook serial numbers. In addition, the crew had to make a logbook entry for every bag that was autoclaved, including the date of sterilization and name of the person who performed the autoclaving. We also indicated the date and time of disposal from the ship, the name of the disposer, and the means of disposal. Daily, as a quality assurance measure, I had to inventory the bags, sharps containers, and logbook. This protocol was followed for the remainder of 1988.

On 02 Jan 89, after a new directive was received from CINCLANTFLT, the hazardous waste disposal plan was revised. Only waste originating from treatment rooms remained classified as PIW; waste from admin, x-ray, and lab spaces was no longer regarded as PIW. This was a start toward a return to common sense.

On 19 Jan 89, after another directive from CINCLANTFLT was issued, a fourth hazardous waste disposal plan was developed and implemented. The only difference from the preceding plan was that non-PIW was now to be subdivided into plastics and nonplastics, with no overboard discharge permitted for plastic waste. Congress had passed a law regulating disposal of plastics at sea. Plastics released into the sea harmed marine life by entanglement or ingestion. They floated and did not biodegrade for hundreds of years. They were a hazard to navigation, especially to small boats since plastics could get caught in propellers.

I was also on the Precious Metals Audit Board ("Gold Board"), which was a group of three officers who regularly met to weigh the precious metals in stock used by the dental lab technicians to ensure that all was accounted for. We used an old-fashioned balance scale to determine the individual pennyweights (dwt) of gold, platinum wire, platinum foil and other alloys.

I was also assigned to the Controlled Medicinals Inventory Board ("Drug Board"), which was a different group of about four officers who regularly met to take inventory of the narcotics and other drugs stocked in the ship's pharmacy. We counted pills one by one and ensured containers were not tampered with.

Peering out over the ocean from the catwalk one night into the black darkness, hearing the ship chop through the water, occasionally catching glimpses of whitewater and tiny flashing lights signaling from ships on the distant horizon, I could not help but be thankful for having had this opportunity to practice dentistry on a United States aircraft carrier. As the recruiting poster (with a photo of a bunch of sailors gazing out across the bow of a small ship at the ocean and some land in the distance) said, "You'll never find another office with a view like this." It was true. The poster went on to state: "While most civilians are striving for a corner office with a window, you already have an office with a view of every corner of the world."

Why did a naval ship need a dental clinic anyway? Aboard the JFK, there was a need to provide dental care for the large crew since the ship, as with the other carriers, was at sea or away from its homeport one-hundred twenty to two-hundred forty days each year, thus preventing crewmembers from having frequent access to dental clinics ashore. Emergencies, of which there was a steady incidence, could be more effectively handled on the ship rather than via some sort of medivac system. And routine dental care helped keep emergencies to a minimum.

In a "Clinical Update" from March of 1987, entitled "Dental Readiness of Our Operating Force," the authors cited statistics emphasizing how dental problems created a high proportion of down time. They stated that "The military's appreciation for dentistry is probably greatest when dental disease unexpectedly results in the loss of personnel or when dental care is limited or unavailable due to operational constraints." They reported that the leading causes of dental emergencies for service personnel were caries and pericoronitis. "An Army after-action report noted that many productive manhours were lost due to the extensive dental treatment needs of Army personnel arriving in Vietnam. In 1968, 80% of dental sick call visits by Army personnel in Vietnam resulted from caries. The incidence of caries-related emergencies in a 1978 Army cold-weather exercise was 52%, and for three Army field exercises conducted in 1981 involving nearly eight-thousand troops, the incidence was 41.2%.

Pericoronitis associated with third molars was the second leading reason for service personnel to seek emergency dental care. "The incidence of pericoronitis-related emergencies experienced among Navy and Marine Corps personnel in Vietnam in 1970 was 18.3%." The authors went on to support the statement that "Although pericoronitis may occur at any time, its incidence may increase when service personnel are confronted with an increasingly stressful environment." The physician on the 1939 Byrd Antarctic expedition reported "Most of our medical problems were teeth."

Also, the article went on to explain, "Dental problems experienced by Vietnam POWs were physically and psychologically debilitating. One former POW stated that although 'a severe toothache may bring about a physical problem slightly detrimental to survival, [it] . . . may produce a psychological condition which, to a prisoner who is isolated, may be extremely hazardous to personal survival.' Thirty-five percent of the POWs told of having had abscesses during their captivity . . ."

So the presence of dental clinics aboard ships served a useful function which assisted in maintaining the readiness of military personnel for engaging in, surviving, and decisively winning war. As the captain would say, "If you can't bite, you can't fight!"

On the 15th of December, 1988, the USS Kennedy returned to Palma. The city was decorated for Christmas, illuminated brightly by hanging lights and decorations over the streets. We stayed until the 19th. It was around this time that I left the six-man stateroom and moved in with LCDR Millar on the third deck. Doug was later to become the head of the Communications Department.

One night in Palma I stayed out very late and by the time I got back to the ship, I was able to get only about an hour of sleep before having to wake up to report to Dental for my day of duty. Fortunately, no patients were scheduled and I only had to treat emergencies as they arose. The good news was that only one patient came in for sick call and all he needed was a simple occlusal adjustment. He had a filling placed the day before, and it had a high spot that needed to be ground down, normally a task that was a walk in the park. As tired as I was, my head fuzzy, I had to devote the entirety of my attention to holding the high speed handpiece at just the right angle so the tooth could be adjusted. I sweated it out as I hit the foot pedal and afterward the patient said his tooth felt "a lot better." And fortunately I did not nick his cheek or tongue in the process. My job done, I retreated to my rack for a couple hours of deep sleep.

What a difference twenty-four hours make. One day a few of us from the ship had a drink at a particular bar and everybody was in great spirits and very friendly. But the next day the mood at that same place turned dark. When we tried to get served, the bartenders ignored us. It soon became very evident that they were going out of their way to avoid us. The crowd did not seem to be as friendly as before. Then one patron began chanting, "Yankee, go home" over and over again, gradually getting louder. I turned to my friend and suggested we get out of there, and we departed. Apparently something happened since the day before to set off the anti-American sentiment. Don't know what it was, but I did know it was time to move along.

Sometimes you get to mingle with the rich and famous. A few officers from the JFK were invited to a luncheon given by some prominent Palma family. The well-to-do attendees were curious as to what we did for a living on the ship. One woman had some TMD issues (TMD stood for temporomandibular disorder, and used to be referred to as TMJ), so in the course of our casual conversations, I supplied her with some tips on what to do for that. Hopefully it helped.

On the 22nd of December, the ship anchored in Cannes, France, the French Riviera city famous for its annual film festival.

We celebrated Christmas while in Cannes. About seven of us from the department formed what someone dubbed the Singing Molar Choir, and sang Christmas songs. We were videotaped by the ship's journalist, to be aired on the local TV channel in Norfolk.

I accompanied one of the ship's officers on a shopping expedition into town. He wanted to find lingerie for his wife, but was a little embarrassed and had a difficult time picking exactly what he wanted. Finally, after what seemed an eternity browsing through multiple boutiques, he at last settled on one particular item. When he brought it to the cashier, however, she said "I'm sorry—it's time for us to close up for lunch. You will have to come back in two hours and I'll ring it up then." Here was another difference between Europe and the United States: in America, the salesperson would have rung up the sale on the spot. In France, the sale did not mean as much as the value of the siesta time.

The United Service Organization (USO) was a nonprofit group with the mission of providing a touch of home for American service personnel. The USO had facilities at more than one-hundred sixty permanent locations worldwide. Since its inception in 1941, the USO sponsored celebrity entertainment shows for deployed personnel. One of these shows was held aboard Kennedy when country music singer Loretta Lynn visited the day after Christmas. She performed with her band and backup singers on a stage erected in the hangar bay.

During our stay in Cannes, I went skiing at a resort in the southern French Alps. To get to the resort required a ride up steep, winding roads into the mountains. During the first day of skiing, Mark Rongone and I had just arrived at the top of a slope from the ski lift when we spotted the pretty French snowbunnies who served as our guides. They were worried because someone from the group had chipped a tooth and they wanted the injured person to see a dentist so he or she could determine if the injury was serious and would need immediate attention. Mark and I looked at each other and said, in the classic line, "We can help. We're dentists."

The snowbunnies were elated. We could be heroes. Taking our poles and pointing our skis downward, we proceeded to fly down the mountainside. Since this was only my second time on downhill skis, I must have wiped out about five times on the way down. But with reckless determination, the dentists arrived at the bottom. When we got to the clubhouse, we checked the tooth and both concurred on the diagnosis—it was no big deal, only a small chip of enamel knocked off some guy's otherwise asymptomatic tooth.

We departed Cannes on New Years Day 1989 and were at sea for the next five days. On one of those days, around noon the Captain's voice came over the 1MC. "This is the Captain speaking. Two of our F-14s were approached in a hostile manner by two Libyan MiGs. Our pilots fired on the MiGs, and splashed both of them. That's all."

I was in my stateroom at my desk when I heard the nonchalant announcement. Doug entered shortly thereafter and I asked him, "Was that announcement what I thought I heard?" He worked in Communications and was up-to-date on all the latest messages. He said yes, this was the real thing.

The incident occurred some seventy miles off the Libyan coast, in international waters. The two F-14s from the USS Kennedy were flying at 20,000 feet on routine patrol when they first picked up the warning from an E-2C Hawkeye radar plane that two Libyan MiG-23s were 72 nautical miles away at 10,000 feet heading directly toward the U.S. planes and the Kennedy. The F-14s located them on their radars, and turned away from the approaching aircraft, a signal that the American pilots were not out to pick a fight. The Libyans, however, "jinked" (shifted abruptly) to the right so as to line up again to head directly toward the U.S. aircrafts. "Bogies appear to be heading directly at us . . ." said one of the American pilots. "Bogies" were any potentially hostile aircraft.

The U.S. fighters turned left and dropped to 3,000 feet, changing directions to the right and then the left. The Libyans matched every turn. "The bogies have jinked back into us now." The Americans turned to the right in another evasive maneuver. Again, the MiGs followed, conveying hostile intent.

After a fifth U.S. avoidance maneuver, one pilot said "the bogies have jinked back at me again for the fifth time. They're on my nose now. Inside of twenty miles." He could wait no longer. "Master arm on . . ." The lead F-14 fired a Sparrow missile at one of the MiGs from a distance of 12 nautical miles. "Fox One. Fox One." It missed, as did another fired seconds later. Fox One was a Sparrow missile; Fox Two was a Sidewinder.

The F-14s split into opposite directions. Both MiGs turned into the path of the wingman on the right, who fired a Sparrow at the trailing plane from only six nautical miles away. The trailing MiG was hit. "Good hit, good hit on one . . . Roger that, good kill, good kill . . . I've got the other one . . . Select Fox Two . . ." The flight leader darted up behind the other MiG and, from only a mere 1.5 miles away, fired a Sidewinder missile, which destroyed the Libyan aircraft. "Let's get out of here," radioed the American pilot. The two Libyan pilots parachuted into the sea. Other pilots would later call this a "knife fight" because the aircraft clashed at unusually close quarters.

The American pilots returned safely to Kennedy. They were quickly debriefed and, we were told, flown immediately to Washington D.C. to report to the President. It was an international event. Newspapers proclaimed: "Two F-14 fighters from the U.S. aircraft carrier John F. Kennedy had been prompted to fire in self-defense after being pursued over international waters by a pair of Libyan MiG-23 fighter jets." The incident made the cover of *TIME* and *Newsweek*.

Libya's leader, Muammar Kaddafi, protested. The carrier was near Crete, more than 120 miles away from recognized Libyan territorial waters when the unexpected combat situation arose.

Soon after, the air crew painted kill symbols (black silhouette of a jet plane) on the aircraft involved in the clash. Two kill symbols were also painted on the ship's superstructure. At least one of the pilots involved in the dogfight was a dental patient of mine.

Two months before the incident, the United States accused Libya of building a vast chemical weapons factory. There was a 1925 Geneva Protocol that banned the use of chemical weapons, but the

United States was concerned that Libya would not hesitate to use what was described as the "poor man's atomic bomb." The suspicion held credence, especially since Libya had been implicated in several terrorist attacks in recent years, among those the midair bombing of Pan Am Flight 103 over Scotland.

The final port call of the Mediterranean Cruise was scheduled to be in Haifa, Israel, but for a time the crew was unsure as to whether or not we would go there, because of the MiG incident. It seemed that flight operations were being carried out more vigorously and for even more sustained durations than was observed previously on the deployment. We wondered what would happen next.

On January 6th, we did, however, anchor at Haifa. Israeli naval boats patrolled around us often. There was increased activity and noise aboard the ship, on the flight deck, and in the water around us, and it was a bit unsettling wondering what was going on.

We stayed in Israel about three days, during which time I took a guided tour. Our bus drove from Haifa in the north in a southerly direction through Tel Aviv, a large modern city. Continuing south, we passed through bleak terrain, which was nothing but sparse scrubby plant growth interspersed upon low-lying empty hills. "Dead tanks" and other disabled military vehicles long ago blown up were left by the roadside as reminders of past battles. We passed Bethlehem, the village where Jesus was born. It looked like a little hamlet off to the side of the road, with spires and domes extending skyward.

We stopped at a kibbutz, which is a communal settlement in Israel. It became apparent that defense of the land was a priority in these villages. We stayed a short while, but then moved on. Next, we visited a roadside restaurant filled with Elvis Presley memorabilia. If you were a fan, you'd be in heaven here. The place was filled with all things Elvis. Then we continued our journey and reached Jerusalem, where we paused on a hillside that offered a spectacular panoramic view of the ancient and sacred grounds. The golden Dome of the Rock, the Moslem center of the city, was a prominent landmark.

Our bus proceeded to Yad Vashem, a museum dedicated to the Nazi holocaust victims. As we entered, we witnessed a large group of very young Israeli soldiers dressed in green uniforms and black combat boots, automatic rifles slung over their shoulders, being admitted to the museum too. Perhaps the scene underscored the sad reality of life in this part of the world: the ever-present imminent danger from attack and need for incessant vigilance. To walk through the chambers of this museum, witnessing the photographs from the concentration camps, especially the ones of the little children, and to listen to each victim's name called out through the darkness of the final room, was to plunge oneself into a profound and hellish nightmare. It elicited disgust for the repulsive depths to which human beings could travel in inflicting harm on others. I think most people emerged from this solemn place altered forever.

We proceeded to the site of the Last Supper. We also visited the Tomb of King David, where we were given temporary yarmulkes to wear before entering the sacred area.

The highlight of our scheduled itinerary was to visit the Old City of Jerusalem. The day before, however, a bomb had exploded there near the Western Wall and our tour guide refused to take us there, being extremely concerned about his own and our safety. But he was pitted against a busload of angry sailors who persisted in protesting, and eventually they convinced him to take us in. He reluctantly parked the bus near a stone wall. "OK, OK . . . We'll go in," he fearfully announced with an annoyed tone. Slowly, cautiously he guided us through the gates to the Old City. He crept along, incessantly looking this way and that, then stopped abruptly and, with a serious face and exaggerated motion of his arm, commanded us to halt and wait where we stood. He then ran ahead to a turn in a high wall along the road, looked in all directions, and then signaled us to hustle forward to catch up with him. "Come on! Come on!" he urged. It was like being in a war movie.

We walked to a place overlooking the Western Wall, commonly called the Wailing Wall, the holiest shrine of the Jewish world. We witnessed people worshipping there. We walked along roads and narrow passageways paved in stone, bordered by stone buildings. It was like something I had never seen before, and it was too bad that we did not get to see the rest. A longer walk would have taken us to places corresponding to the sites represented in Christianity's Stations of the Cross. Instead, our guide had had enough and, as he wiped the heavy perspiration off his forehead, he gave us the word that we would now return to the bus, no more Old City.

So we departed safely. On the ride back to fleet landing, we stopped at a diamond center where we observed diamond cutters at work and could purchase rocks at low prices. Some sailors were planning engagements and such, and so several diamonds were sold. Back near fleet landing, I had a falafel, a popular type of sandwich.

Aboard the ship, I treated two embassy officials, who were apparently eligible for dental care. The next day, on the 9th of January, the USS Kennedy departed Israel.

We would be at sea for the remainder of the deployment. During this time, the aircraft carrier USS Theodore Roosevelt pulled alongside our ship. A handful of us from Dental donned cranials and hearing protectors and flew over to the ship in a helo. We came in for a smooth landing aboard the Roosevelt's flight deck. Inside the nuclear-powered aircraft carrier was a much more spacious dental department than ours, so large that I must have exclaimed, "Oh my god, you could play basketball here!" We passed along hints we felt might be useful to the crew that was to relieve us in the Med. We ate lunch in their wardroom, after which we flew back to our ship.

One day as we were crossing the Atlantic Ocean, I looked out over the stern of the ship from a vantage point near my battle dressing station. I saw several "small boys," which were the Navy ships much smaller than carriers. They were members of the Kennedy Battle Group plowing through the choppy seas, also heading back to the United States in completion of the deployment. I was amazed at how much they pitched and yawed, their bows crashing through the water ahead, temporarily submerging. They had accompanied us throughout the Med Cruise, although we had different ports of call at any one time and so did not actually see much of each other. If a crisis developed, however, all the ships in the battle group could swiftly be recalled to converge together as a single formidable force. What an awesome sight it was to see all these warships travelling together in such close proximity to the USS Kennedy, moving through the ocean as an integrated carrier battle group.

The Kennedy battle group was commanded by Rear Admiral David R. Morris and included the Kennedy, guided-missile cruisers Bainbridge and Biddle, frigates Truett and McCandless and the oiler Platte, all from Norfolk; the guided-missile destroyer MacDonough, destroyer John Rodgers and ammunition ship Santa Barbara, all from Charlestown, South Carolina; the frigate Cannole from Newport, Rhode Island; and the frigates Voge and McInerney, both from Mayport, Florida.

The Mediterranean Amphibious Readiness Group, led by the Guam, also included the amphibious transport dock Nashville, dock-landing ship Pensacola, tank-landing ship Fairfax County and amphibious cargo ship Charlestown, all based in Norfolk.

The Norfolk-based destroyer tender Yellowstone operated independently in the Mediterranean.

During the deployment, I performed eight-hundred eleven T2 exams, nearly one-thousand total amalgam surfaces, over one-hundred composites, and handed out sixty prescriptions and obturated forty root canals. Over one-hundred quadrants of scaling and root planing were done. There were many emergency procedures, extractions and some crown and bridge accomplished. In addition, there were other miscellaneous procedures that I did.

Near the end of January, I had to fly off the carrier in a helo to Bermuda to make room aboard the ship for a tech rep to come aboard to study the wear and tear on the carrier's mechanical systems. Many of the ship's personnel were flown off like that a few days earlier before the Kennedy was to arrive home. I walked around on the island of Bermuda for a few hours before catching a military flight back to Norfolk. The Mediterranean Sea Cruise had ended.

PART FIVE

MORE DEPLOYMENTS
AND EVOLUTIONS

After the half-year deployment, the ship went into a cool-down mode. Many of her crew went on leave. Family relationships were reestablished. In Dental, the makeup of the staff gradually changed as, one by one, personnel moved on to either new duty stations or the civilian sector while new faces arrived. The whole atmosphere within the department changed, not for better or for worse; it was just different.

The ship "went into the yards" for a few weeks for an industrial overhaul at the Norfolk Naval Shipyard. I returned to living in my Virginia Beach apartment, reengaging in the daily Road Warrior commute. I had to park my car a distance from where the ship was moored inside the shipyard and allow extra time for the long walk in. During this shipyard period we were permitted to come to work and leave in civilian clothes. I walked alongside the yardbirds each day. Shipyard workers stood out in stark contrast to the Navy personnel. They tended to look rough, often with long hair and tattered and soiled clothes. They were hardworking, patriotic Americans I was glad to have on our side.

One day as I hiked with a confident and swift stride to the ship, dressed in blue jeans and boots, carrying a backpack over my shoulder, with Bruce Springsteen's *Badlands* and *The Promised Land* bellowing in my ears and pumping me up, I thought: *Isn't this a great job! A few weeks ago I was working in a dental office in the middle of the Atlantic Ocean, and today I get to hike to that same dental office which is now surrounded by land and completely different scenery!* This variety certainly kept the job interesting. It seemed a much better deal than having to go to the same old landlocked office day in and day out as I would if I had a civilian practice.

Aboard the stationary ship, thick electric cords, flexible tubing, metal pipes and tools crisscrossed and littered many passageways. There were peculiar, compressible vinyl ventilation tubes about a foot in diameter found in certain areas where increased air flow was needed by the workers. There was a lot of noise, but fortunately not as much as I experienced one time ago when I visited the USS Coral Sea's dental spaces when that ship was in the yard. Their staff had to practice dentistry under more difficult conditions, as banging and vibrations completely surrounded them, pounding out like from one massive machine shop.

In time, we left the yards behind and returned to sea in June for four days, and then five more days the following week for more *sea trials*. By this time I had inherited many more collateral duties, including the job of Division Officer, which kept me extremely busy.

In July, we went out to sea for about two weeks. During this time a fire broke out in the main spaces but was quickly extinguished.

LCDR Wallace was preparing to leave the ship, and his replacement, CDR George Hull, reported aboard to take his place as Department Head. They had a couple weeks of cross-over during the transition, during which they exchanged valuable information. One evening, I stood with the two department heads by the chain fence at the edge of the hangar and gazed at the Miami skyline, brightly illuminated on the horizon.

Throughout 1989, new dentists reported aboard the ship. In April, LT Stephen Pachuta arrived. In August, LT Jeff Clark and LCDR Dave Jennings checked in.

About a half-dozen women sailors were brought aboard the USS Kennedy with *TAD* orders (temporary duty) one week while we were at sea. They had some special project to participate in. Having them aboard was a unique event because aircraft carrier crews at the time were all-male; it would not be until the 1990's when women would be routinely assigned duty aboard these ships. Well, as it turned out, a young male sailor appeared in my chair for a dental exam. I saw in his chart that he had just had his annual T2 exam last month, so I asked him, "Why are you here again? You just had an exam!" The nineteen-year old shook his head and grinned, and shared with me how he and a friend snuck by the Marine guards assigned to watch over the female sailors. He and his buddy hid in the back of the girls' lockers, trying to sneak a peek, I guess. One of the girls discovered their whereabouts, however. The hapless patient explained that "The girl who grabbed me was big and muscular! I couldn't get away. She dragged me to the Marine. The Marines eventually caught my friend, too. We got sent to Captain's Mast, and the Captain kicked us out of the Navy." So I had to do the separation dental exam on this unhappy sailor.

One day as the ship's dentists were eating lunch together, some guy we had never seen before just magically appeared, sauntering in to the wardroom, taking a seat next to us. He spoke as if we had known him forever, relating the tale of how he had just been flown aboard the ship in an arrested landing upon the flight deck. He looked a bit worn out from all the travel. We found out that he was a Navy Reserve dentist, CDR Bob DeMaggio from Massachusetts, who would spend two weeks with us. He performed dentistry, kept us entertained with his jokes, and took all kinds of pictures. He was the ultimate tourist, getting to places on the ship that I never even saw during the entire time I lived there.

One of the unique places the good commander got to see was deep down inside the engineering spaces in the Auxiliary Machinery Room. There, on the steel bulkhead, was a beautiful mural of "Christ Calming the Seas." The artwork was a reproduction of the famous painting by Rembrandt. As the story goes, a young second class machinist mate who was attached to the Kennedy in her early years at sea was inspired by Rembrandt's painting. The petty officer spent many hours of his free time, when he wasn't lubricating machine gears and parts or painting the bulkhead. The Chief Engineering Officer at the time recognized the young man's ability, and also enjoyed art, so the mural project was allowed to go to completion. Eventually the artist left the military, but his art persisted. Sailors working in the Engineering Department have guarded the mural, protecting it from damage and carefully touching up any chipped areas when necessary. Whenever heavy-duty overhaul work was performed, the mural was carefully covered with blankets and wood framing to protect it.

The circumstances under which I was able to serve as a dental professional aboard a naval vessel unfolded slowly over the years. Writings from long ago indicated that nautical medicine probably had its beginnings with the seafaring ancient Greeks, Phoenicians and Romans. After the fall of Rome and during the Middle Ages, little was documented concerning the presence of medical personnel on ships. It was known, however, that the maritime republics of Genoa and Venice established something akin to "Medical Corps" that provided physicians not only aboard ships but also "in the castles and shore stations beyond the sea."

The use of sail and further development of navigation eventually made longer voyages possible. The long periods at sea brought the need for dentists as well as physicians who would go to sea aboard ships.

In the United States, Edward Maynard was given the credit for being the first to advocate military dentistry. This happened in 1844. Dr. Maynard was a Washington, DC dentist whose practice included several presidents of the United States and many national figures of the time. During those days, dental treatment in the military was conducted by medical personnel whose training was not overly concerned with the practice of dentistry. Dr. Maynard's aim was to improve the health of military personnel by requiring military healthcare providers to possess a more thorough knowledge of the practice of dentistry. His initiatives provoked much discussion, but were met with rejections and other obstacles. It was not until 1873 that the first dentist was appointed to serve as an officer in the U.S. Navy. He was Thomas O. Walton, DDS, of Annapolis, Maryland.

He was appointed to work at the Naval Academy, providing dental care for the midshipmen.

It was in that same year that a Navy medical inspector made the following comment: "The hair, beard, and teeth are all neglected on board ship. It would be a difficult matter to compel old sailors to cleanse their teeth, but all the boys should be obliged to purchase tooth brushes, and to use them regularly."

In 1879 a dental examination became a part of the physical exam for applicants seeking entrance into the Navy. The following year, in 1880, Congress decided to replace the position of dental officer with a contract dentist, who would be paid a salary of $1,600 per year. Thomas Walton became the first contract dentist working for the Navy.

In 1886, instructions for Medical Officers of the United States Navy described the following dental equipment:

Dental Case #1
1 Upper bicuspid forceps
1 Lower incisor forceps
1 Right upper molar forceps
1 Left upper molar forceps
1 Lower molar forceps for both sides
1 Wisdom tooth forceps (bayonet)
1 Front-root forceps
1 Back-root forceps (bayonet)
2 Elevators
1 Gum lancet

Many more urgings were given by various sources to establish a Navy Dental Corps, but resistance was strong.

In 1903, the Surgeon General first made mention of the use of hospital stewards who had training and experience in dentistry. He stated that these men were providing dental care at the following sites: Training Station in Newport, Rhode Island; aboard the receiving ship, Columbia; at the Naval Station, Guam. He stated further that arrangements were being made for dental service by hospital stewards on the receiving ships, Wabash and Franklin, and at the Training Station, San Francisco, California.

In 1904, Edward Earl Harris, DDS, became the first graduate dentist to enlist in the USN as a hospital steward performing dental services exclusively.

In 1907, the Surgeon General vehemently continued his requests for the establishment of a Dental Corps. He cited the need for dental treatment, the suffering resulting from the lack of such treatment, and even instances of death attributed to dental disease. Portions of his report are quoted as follows: "Much of the tonsillitis and pharyngitis in the Navy can be traced to bad teeth . . . it may be added that a bad tooth . . . may even endanger life . . . . The patient had an ulcerated tooth . . . and the man died thirty-six hours later. Another fatality . . . developed from gangrene of the nerve of a molar tooth . . . . At many of our stations and on our ships dental attention . . . is not available, and the consequences are great suffering and disability and impairment of efficiency. A bill has been drafted and submitted, September 20, 1907 . . . and it is earnestly recommended that Congress be asked in its coming session to take favorable action on it."

In 1908, Dr. Richard Grady, the dentist who had replaced Dr. Walton at the Naval Academy, presented a paper entitled, "The Dentist in the United States Navy: An Account of the Efforts to Secure a Dental Corps." Dentistry in the Navy was described as follows: *Government ships are provided with dental cases, each containing a set of forceps, elevators, evacuators, engine burs, plastic filling instruments, and high-grade gutta percha. These are used by the surgeons and hospital stewards, some of whom have taken courses in dentistry. Practically there is no room on ships for dental work, for chair, cabinet, engine, etc. If located in or near the sick bay, as the hospital is termed on a man-of-war, the dentist could work on bright days only. As to living quarters there might be trouble. Recognizing that the equipment of the general surgeon is not wholly adequate to relieve the diseases incident to the mouth, teeth, and jaws, the Navy, having no dental corps, as you know, Surgeon General Rixey has provided a course of lectures in the Naval Medical School in Washington for officers of the Medical Corps of the Navy. These are on elementary dentistry and instruction in the treatment of ordinary dental troubles, including relief from suffering, the insertion of temporary fillings to protect teeth from further decay until a favorable opportunity can be secured for permanent work, and the extraction of teeth.*

Indicating the need for dentistry, the fleet surgeon of the Pacific Fleet reported work accomplished during the period 28 Apr-28 Aug 09 as follows: *On the Tennessee . . . 282 teeth were crowned and bridged, 180 devitalized and 27 extracted; . . . there were 219 gold fillings, 412 amalgam fillings, and 67 cement fillings. This work cost the crew $2960 and represents only a part of what was desired, as a dentist could have been kept busy for an additional number of months, but was unable to continue owing to the departure of the ship . . . .*

Around 1910, there were about a dozen hospital stewards with a dental degree who were performing dental services only. The Surgeon General reported to the Secretary of the Navy that at the Navy Yard in Philadelphia *In the absence of the provision for dental surgeons for the navy a civilian dentist has continued to work at the barracks at stated hours . . . . At present he is obliged to work in the wash room, which is unsuitable.*

All of the momentum started by Dr. Maynard back in 1844 reached fruition in 1912 when Congress authorized the Navy Dental Corps. The first dental officer appointed to serve in the U.S. Navy Dental Corps was Emory A. Bryant, DDS of Washington, D.C. The first dental officer to report aboard ship was Dr. Harry E. Harvey on March 5, 1913, aboard the USS Solace where he served until October 1915. The first dental officer ordered to an oversea base was Dr. James L. Brown, ordered to the US Naval Station, Guam on April 27th of 1913. The first dental officer ordered to Marine duty was Dr. Lucian C. Williams, reporting to Parris Island, South Carolina on August 4, 1913.

In October of 1916, the Secretary of the Navy reported that *The Dental Corps is a new experiment in the Navy and its usefulness will be better demonstrated as time goes on and its influence upon the personnel of the Navy has had time to accumulate.*

The first Naval Dental Corps officer to die while engaged in a combat situation was LtJG Weeden E. Osborne during World War I. He was awarded the Medal of Honor *For extraordinary heroism in actual conflict with the enemy and under fire, during the advance on Bouresches in France . . . in helping to carry the wounded to a place of safety. While engaged in this heroic duty he was killed. He was at the time attached to the 6th Regiment, U.S. Marines.*

Another Navy dental officer, LCDR Cornelius H. Mack was awarded the Navy Cross in 1918: *For extraordinary heroism and devotion to duty with the 6th Regiment, U.S. Marines. In the action at Bois de Belleau (France) . . . . when his dressing station was subject to a heavy gas bombardment, he remained on duty and carried on the evacuation of the wounded, refusing to leave until all wounded and Hospital Corps men had been removed to a place of safety; as a result he was severely gased. In the action at Vierzy [France], on July 19, 1918, he accompanied the advance and was exposed for fifteen hours to the fire of machine guns and artillery, performing his duties with marked coolness and precision.*

From a total of thirty-five Navy dentists on duty before the outbreak of World War I, the Navy Dental Corps grew to over five-hundred. Of forty-three transports used during the war, twenty-two carried a dental officer. Captain H.T. Daniels described his duty aboard the transport USS Mongolia as changing and applying dressings, administering anesthetics, and performing many other duties of the sick bay. CDR George C. Fowler of the Navy Dental Corps described being torpedoed one night two-hundred miles off the coast of France while aboard the USS Covington and being rescued by the destroyer USS Smith.

As early as 1923 the Fleet Surgeon, U.S. Pacific Fleet stated in his report to the Surgeon General: *In the air squadrons, for the purpose of anticipating trouble . . . and with a view to eliminating every possible cause for impairment of the sense of coordination, it has been urged that intensive attention to the teeth of flying crews be given, and that a system of dental inspection with follow up observation and treatment be established.*

On February 3, 1923 the U.S. Naval Dental School opened to provide postgraduate instruction to Dental Corps officers and to train hospital corpsmen to serve as dental assistants and hygienists.

In July of 1923 the first proposal for a casualty care training program in the Dental Corps was made.

In 1924 the Surgeon General described a course at the Naval Dental School which dealt with *the collateral duties of dental officers: This course is considered especially important as all newly commissioned dental officers are assigned to the school. In the days prior to the establishment of the School, a dental officer was often sent directly upon receiving his appointment to independent duty. He was unfamiliar with naval customs and was thrown in contact with senior officers to whom a dental officer was a new problem and who could not be expected to understand his needs or appreciate the difficulty of the situation.*

In 1925 the Surgeon General first mentioned the treatment of veterans by the Dental Corps. In 1926 came the first mention of establishing dental operating rooms aboard ship. In 1936 an attempt was made to increase the number of dental officers at navy yards *so that personnel aboard ships without a dental officer may receive treatment when in port.*

In 1938 an article, *What Surprised Me about the Soviets*, written by LT Curtiss W. Schantz of the Navy Dental Corps was published. The essay analyzed the current social life of the Soviet culture and was written following a visit of the USS Augusta to Vladivostok while the lieutenant was the Dental Officer aboard that ship.

The Navy Dental Corps gradually grew over the years, from 31 officers in 1915 to 1,683 on active duty in 1982. With its growth came significant technological developments. Innovations included experimental models of portable dental units that could be used at sea to provide dental treatment aboard ships that were not equipped with dental operatories. Mobile dental vans which could be parked pierside to serve the needs of sailors and marines wherever necessary were experimented with and the first self-contained mobile dental operating unit was placed in operation on February 18, 1945. The Navy Dental Corps participated in the 1973 experiment in which two-way closed-circuit television telecommunication via satellite was established, linking Washington, D.C. with the hospital ship S.S. Hope in Alagoas, Brazil.

It was the Navy Dental Corps that contributed greatly to the development of the high-speed handpiece which revolutionized the whole field of dentistry after World War Two. It had become evident that diamond and carbide burs performed best at the highest speeds available and that increased speeds were needed for even more effective cutting. Complicated pulley arrangements had been designed which diminished the vibrations transferred to the patient, thus decreasing some of the discomfort. But it was not until handpieces were air-driven that speeds of 300,000 rpm could be attained. This made dental restoration easier for the patient to bear, and easier for the dentist to perform, thus augmenting the quality of care. The pioneer models of the dental air turbine developed by the Navy were significant developments in the history of dentistry.

During the attack on Pearl Harbor at the outbreak of WWII, two officers of the Navy Dental Corps were killed: LCDR Hugh R. Alexander on the USS Oklahoma and LCDR Thomas E. Crowley on the USS Arizona. Four were wounded. Ten dental officers were assigned to the Navy Yard and they reported to the dispensary and assisted in the care of the wounded as they arrived. Dental technicians were sent out on rescue teams to ships and various areas of the harbor. Some two-hundred dentures were lost during the attack. Some of these were lost in ships that sunk, but a large majority of them were lost in the oil-covered water when the wearers became sick from ingesting the oil.

During the war, a critical shortage of dental materials was developing and so it was directed that used burs *be saved, cleaned, dried, oiled, and sent to the U.S. Naval Medical Supply Depot, Brooklyn, New York, for resharpening and reissue.* Also, directives were issued ordering the *saving of amalgam scrap, precious metal bench sweepings and polishing residue.*

In addition to the two dental officers killed at Pearl Harbor, there were about fifteen more who lost their lives in combat situations during the remainder of the war, most of them while aboard ships. Four Navy dental officers died as prisoners of war. Nine Navy dental officers who had been captured as prisoners of war by the Japanese were returned to the United States following cessation of the war. About thirty-one Navy dental officers were wounded in action.

During WWII the following dental work was accomplished by the Navy Dental Corps: 29,654,343 dental restorations; 509,292 dentures; 27,232 bridges; 4,229,809 teeth extracted; 8,097 fractures treated.

Dental clinic ships were recommended by the Commander, Service Force, U.S. Pacific Fleet in 1945, and in August of that same year four such ships were authorized. The war ended, however, and the plans were scrapped.

Soon after the war, the Japanese General, Hideki Tojo, considered one of the chief architects and perpetrators of the Pacific war, was apprehended by Allied Forces and imprisoned in Tokyo's Sugamo Prison, where he became a patient of a young Navy dentist, LtJG Jack Mallory. General Tojo was awaiting his war crimes trial, his teeth were examined, and it was determined he would need to have all his remaining upper teeth extracted because of advanced periodontal disease and other destruction. Then a full denture would be constructed. When the general was escorted to the dental clinic by two or three guards, Dr. Mallory noted that he appeared as a "rather tired, grandfatherly, innocuous-looking little old Japanese man." The denture was made and, in addition to applying the patient's name on the acrylic, Dr. Mallory used a dental round bur to inscribe in Morse code dots and dashes along the border the words "Remember Pearl Harbor." At first only a few people knew about it, but the secrecy did not last long. News reporters heard about the prank and were soon knocking on the door. Dr. Mallory was ordered by his C.O. to grind the message out. So on the night of Valentine's Day 1947, he drove twelve miles in a snowstorm to the prison and obliterated the Morse code message by grinding with a heatless stone and joe-dandy disks. Nothing more was heard about the denture as the news story died down. Dr. Mallory last saw the General in the courtroom during his trial. He recalled how General Tojo kept staring at him as if saying to himself, "I know that guy from somewhere." In Dr. Mallory's own words: "He studied me for what seemed a long time and finally his eyes lit up and he broke into a big smile. Pointing a finger to his teeth, he bowed toward me in a gesture of thank you, which was nice on his part."

During the Korean War, the Navy Cross was awarded posthumously to DN Thomas Andrew Christenson, Jr: *For extraordinary heroism while serving with a Marine Railroad Train Guard, attached to the First Amphibian Tractor Battalion, during operations against enemy aggressor forces in Korea, on 06 November 1950. With the train ambushed by a greatly outnumbering hostile guerilla force while temporarily halted under cover of darkness at Kowon, Christenson boldly exposed himself to intense enemy machine-gun, grenade, and small-arms fire to rescue the wounded and administer first aid. Despite severe wounds sustained while helping a stricken comrade, he bravely continued in his valiant efforts as the enemy closed in from all directions. Mortally wounded by vicious hostile fire delivered at point-blank range, Christenson, by his superb courage, self-sacrificing efforts on behalf of his comrades, and unswerving devotion to duty, served to inspire all who observed him, thereby reflecting the highest credit upon himself and the United States Naval Service.*

From July 1, 1951 to February 29, 1952, sixty-three thousand eight-hundred fifty-seven patients received "front line" dentistry in Korea, either in trucks that had been converted to mobile dental units or in Quonset huts. This was necessitated because of the change in the basic combat mission of the Marine Corps during the war.

The Vietnam War brought about an increased need for oral surgery support to the Marine Corps. During the war, Naval Dental Corps personnel served Marine Corps units by providing general dentistry support under all conditions. The dental detachments ranged from several personnel operating in southeast Asian huts or old French buildings in Chu Lai, DaNang, Phu Bia, or Quang Tri, to one dental officer and a dental technician in mobile or fixed dental clinics in Khe Sahn, Cua Viet, Con Thien, or An Hoa. In addition, DC personnel voluntarily rendered humanitarian aid to Vietnamese civilians. At the peak period in Vietnam, there were approximately 78 dental officers and 170 dental technicians assigned to support the

Marines. In all, approximately 335 dental officers and 835 dental technicians served in Vietnam.

Now that I digressed to elucidate what had transpired over time to enable dentists to stow their equipment as well as themselves aboard ships, I'll return to more deployments and evolutions of the USS Kennedy following her Mediterranean Sea expedition. In July of 1989, the Soviet Union sent three warships to the United States for a friendly port call. In turn, the United States would send warships to the USSR later in the year. This was historic in that it was only the second time since the end of World War Two that the Soviet Navy and United States exchanged visits. The Cold War had begun to thaw.

Approximately 1100 personnel from the Soviet Navy arrived aboard the Slava class guided missile cruiser Marshal Ustinov, the Sovremenny class destroyer Oilichny and the Boris Chilkin class oiler Genrikh Gasanov for a four-day port visit. The ships berthed at Pier 7 of the Norfolk Naval Base, not far from the Kennedy.

The crew of USS Kennedy prepared the ship for a two-hour tour offered to the Soviet sailors. All Kennedy personnel dressed in their snow-white summer white uniforms. Hundreds of Soviet personnel received guided tours of the spaces aboard Kennedy. As I strode swiftly across the flight deck, my foot inadvertently was trapped by one of the arresting cables. In an uncontrolled crash I landed, my clean white uniform now blemished with a large black greasy stain. I finished what I was doing, all the while conscious of and trying to hide the oil slick on my pant leg. The first chance I got, I retired to my stateroom below decks for a change of clothes.

Only limited numbers of American personnel could tour the Soviet ships, so our department drew straws to see who would get to go. I was one of the winners and went aboard the Marshal Ustinov, which was very different from any American naval ship I had ever seen. It was like an alien vessel, with giant missile tubes arranged symmetrically on the port and starboard sides. A long narrow corridor lay between the tubes and inboard superstructure. The color of the deck was something like an orange-brown. The radar looked as if it were from Star Wars. At 613 feet long and

12,500 tons, she was bigger than her closest American counterpart, the 7,650-ton, 533-foot USS Harry E. Yarnell. There were spaces of plush carpeting, and there even was a bar. The ship's function was anti-ship warfare. Its giant missiles were intended to destroy American aircraft carriers like the USS Kennedy.

The Soviet officers wore uniforms that made them look like they were on vacation in the Caribbean, with their yellow shirts untucked, left to hang down outside their black, white or yellow pants, like Cuban guayaberas. The Soviet sailors wore long-sleeved uniforms of all white or white shirt/black pants. The shirt had a V-shaped collar with blue and white stripes. When asked if it was uncomfortable to be in the hot 90-degree heat of a Norfolk summer, they said yes, that they had not yet adapted to the climate. In fact, they claimed there was snow on the ground July 5th when they departed their homeport of Severomorsk near the Arctic Circle in Lapland.

Propaganda in the form of photos, diagrams, and posters was carefully arranged for display about the decks. One poster said: "Our Motherland—the USSR" and had pictures of Mikhail Gorbachov, a Soviet woman clad in a colorful ethnic costume, and street scenes with beautiful buildings.

A typical meal aboard their ship was borscht and stewed fruit. While at sea, they played chess or checkers, watched movies on the VCR or TV, listened to records, and sang songs in the mess decks to the accompaniment of the guitar or accordion.

Americans learned a lot about their enemies during the visit. The Soviets loved McDonald's french fries. The average age of the sailors was 19-and-single. They were overwhelmed by American stores, claiming they were impressed by how everything was well-organized and easy to find. They were amazed at how many colors of paint were available. I was presented with a pamphlet about "The Soviet Navy" and a book about World War Two printed in Russian.

Commanding the Soviet warships was Vice Admiral Igor V. Kasatonov, who reported that the Soviet sailors "were very nervous" about coming to the United States and spent a long time preparing for it. When asked how the two navies could cooperate more in the future, Kasatonov said each nation could send observers to the other's military exercises, there could be more port visits, and there could be greater contacts between naval specialists including doctors. And that concludes my personal account of this visit between Cold War antagonists. From this departure, we will gallop to the end of the book atop the series of brief anecdotes which follow.

One day my car was doused with overspray. It was parked near the JFK, off the pier just to the port side of the bow which was pointed inland. The ship was being spray-painted at the time and most of my car's exterior received paint droplets from the aerosol carried by the wind. Unfortunately I did not have the car protected by a cloth covering I sometimes used. I had to get the vehicle buffed.

In August of 1989 the ship went to sea for three weeks. By this time I had my hands full as Division Officer. One of the dental technicians tested positive for marijuana, and drug paraphernalia was discovered in the dental operatory where he worked. The things I learned at OIS came back to me when I had to prepare the legal paperwork and go through Captain's Mast with him. Another dental technician, who had only recently checked aboard, went UA. He also owed hundreds of dollars to the Senior Chief and owed $133 to a video rental store for overdue video tapes. He missed two ship's movements, in addition to numerous other infractions. We tried to work with him, giving him financial counseling and such, but he failed to respond and just kept messing up even more. I had to go to Captain's Mast with him too. He was to be separated from the Navy.

During the August deployment we made a port call in Fort Lauderdale, Florida. While there, a 5K run was held on the flight deck and we soaked up the hot sun on the beaches. Wet tee shirt contests seemed to abound.

In September there was a Dependent's Day Cruise in which the ship got underway for a few hours with family members of the crew invited to come aboard to tour the Kennedy and watch limited flight operations. Wives, siblings, mothers and fathers were able to observe flight ops from bleachers set up on the flight deck.

In October we got underway for two weeks, during which time one of our F-14s crashed into the ocean off the stern of the ship. Fortunately the pilot and RIO were rescued. More bad news, however, came the following day: "Plane in the water . . ." was the message conveyed over the 1MC. This was the S-3 Viking incident described in the Introduction.

A week later, the ship pulled in to Portland, Maine for about three days, during which time we shopped at L.L. Bean's and stopped in Kennebunkport to catch a glimpse of President Bush's oceanside home on Walker's Point. A year later, when I would be stationed at the Portsmouth Naval Shipyard in New Hampshire, I treated many Coast Guard personnel. They told me tales of how, during their assignment to protect the Commander-in-Chief whenever he went for a ride in his lightning-fast cigarette boat, President Bush would playfully outmaneuver them. He would head in one direction with the Coast Guard following, but then would suddenly dart off in a different direction, losing them in the process.

At the end of October, we deployed again, this time for nearly three weeks on the OPPE cruise. The acronym meant Operation Propulsion Plant Examination. This was the big test for the Engineering Department, to evaluate its responses to all operational commitments. Inspectors came aboard to scrutinize the electrical safety, heat stress and hearing conversation programs. They analyzed the damage control repair lockers, engine and machinery spaces, watchstander knowledge, fire lighting capability and materiel readiness.

One of my duties was as Supply Officer. Duties included tasks such as: establishing a financial budget for the fiscal year, maintaining records of which high-speed handpieces were issued to each doctor, keeping inventory, monitoring expiration-dated items, and ordering, receiving, storing and issuing supplies. I worked with our Supply Petty Officer, both of us discovering it was not always easy to maneuver through the difficult military supply system.

Back in the homeport, I decided to remove from the ship several old handpieces and hand instruments that no one was ever going to use aboard the ship. Perhaps they could be redistributed throughout the Navy Dental Corps, so I transferred them to the Fleet Dental Officer in Norfolk.

On another occasion, I removed sixty-four oral surgery forceps which had accumulated over the years in the dental supply storage spaces inside the ship's focsl (forecastle). Do you know how much all of those weighed? By removing them from the ship, I'm sure the carrier's miles-per-gallon increased significantly. I put the hefty instruments, used for extracting teeth, into a large box which I carried off the ship one afternoon. The box was very heavy. As I struggled to the spot where I had parked my car earlier in the day, I noticed the automobile was no longer there. I put the box down and checked with some dockworker to see if he knew what had happened. He said "Yeah, some cars was towed today. Used to be you could park there, but today they says that changed." I spotted a tiny "No Parking" sign, barely legible. My choice was to hike all the way back to the ship with the heavy load of tooth pliers or leave the box on the sidewalk and hope no one would steal the $2,000 worth of merchandise while I jogged the two miles to the automobile pound. No one was around who could give me a lift. I decided to just hike with the box to the pound.

After I regained my car, I drove to the Naval Dental Center. Lugging the box of forceps inside, I set my overweight package down on the deck and knocked on the Fleet Dental Officer's office door. He said, "Come in. Can I help you?" I said I had brought him some dental tools that I hoped he could redistribute throughout the fleet. When I lifted the box and brought it into the room, I cannot say he looked thrilled. He suddenly became very serious, with a most concerned expression on his face, and instructed me to lay it down in the corner. At first he appeared unsure of what he really wanted to say next, but eventually said, "Thanks a lot," as if to say "Now what am I supposed to do with that? Thanks for the extra work."

DN Willie Gibson, or "Gibs" as we called him, was my assistant for a time. He did a good job, but there were days when he'd actually fall asleep while suctioning for my high speed handpiece and I'd have to nudge him. One time he was even drooling, probably as he was entering into a deeper zone of sleep. It seems he was spending a lot of time at late-night partying and not getting enough sleep when we were in our homeport. But even so, he was a good guy who just needed a little guidance. The Dental Department received a message that we could send someone to the school to become a prophy technician. I recommended him but I was met by resistance from the skeptics in our department. Nevertheless, I had faith he could do well in that program and pushed for him. He got accepted and passed the classes and returned to Kennedy to be a crackerjack dental prophy tech.

As the department's Safety Officer, I was responsible for things such as the following: ensuring all electrical equipment, like irons, cassette players and razors, were safety-checked and tagged; ensuring adequate quantities of EEBD's were present in our spaces and personnel were trained in their use; conducting egress drills with newly-reported staff; posting emergency phone numbers throughout the department; conducting Code Blue medical emergency drills; ensuring drugs and equipment in the spark kit were not expired or faulty; ensuring personnel were current in their CPR certification; ensuring that the staff used protective lenses when necessary; identifying and correcting any tripping/slipping hazards; conducting regular maintenance on equipment to minimize defects that could lead to injuries; ensuring the eye-wash stations were ready for emergency use; running the radiation safety program; directing the fire safety program; disposing of hazardous material; training personnel in safety issues; and familiarizing new staff members with the entire safety program.

I had by now come to know that to be an officer meant that in addition to performing your job of being a dentist, you were also to be very much aware that you were an integral part of the war machine as you contributed your efforts to maintain high dental readiness. In addition, you assumed many more responsibilities that were tied in to the overall mission of the U.S. Armed Forces. You were a manager, leader, social worker, and big brother, and you held a variety of collateral duties. As an officer, you were responsible for directing your own actions as well as the troops in a way that facilitated success toward fulfilling the mission of the Armed

Forces. If you began to forget this, you really were no longer a naval officer.

On the 30th of November 1989 the ship deployed for nearly two weeks on REFTRA, which was "Refresher Training." This was a rough, challenging experience ships had to go through in their workup cycle. The Kennedy steamed toward GITMO (Guantanamo Bay, Cuba) and the Caribbean Sea to accomplish REFTRA. We spent extensive periods of time every day at general quarters. I also began the monumental task of deciphering the menagerie of parts listed on the CCOLs (Compartment Check-Off Lists) which Dental was responsible for. These lists had to do with damage-control items such as firemain valves, deck drains, washdown systems, and various circuits and gauges. I was only a dentist, so it was a challenge just to find all the components and ensure they were satisfactory. There was a whole new CCOL language to learn. I spent countless hours in a dirty uniform crawling under the pipes into compressed spaces, armed with flashlight and clipboard. I was able to map out the location of each component, drawing color-coded schematic diagrams which I hoped would have been useful to persons who would need to go over this in the future.

Many of the CCOL parts were at the entranceway hatch to the dental spaces, in the main passageway on the 2nd deck. Having spent much time there tackling this project, I was able to observe that there was, at most times, a nearly constant flow of pedestrian traffic through this area and, although some faces looked familiar, it seemed that most of the people I did not know. This attested to the enormity of the ship's population. It truly was a floating city, unlike the smaller Navy ships on which everybody knew everyone else.

In December of 1989, the Secretary of the Navy awarded the Meritorious Unit Commendation to the USS Kennedy battle group for the 1988-89 Mediterranean Sea deployment. The ships involved were recognized for their outstanding execution of numerous exercises with our allies, favorable contributions to our foreign relations, and "unparalleled combat readiness."

We began the new year of 1990 deploying for over five continuous weeks on the Advanced Phase Cruise. This was a higher intensity workup phase during which the ship was called upon to exercise all warfighting capabilities. The scenarios included war-at-sea strikes, bombing and strafing runs, air raids, anti-submarine warfare, and anti-air warfare exercises.

Concurrently we were also prepared to engage in "drug-ops," but this got cancelled. The efforts of the United States to diminish the infiltration of illegal drugs into the homeland nearly entered a phase in which aircraft carriers were going to begin patrolling off the coast of South America, working with other Navy and Coast Guard vessels to impede the drug traffic going north.

We made a port call to Mayport, Florida of nearly a week long. I checked out the Kennedy Space Center and Epcot Center. I performed a T2 exam using a plastic mirror on Daisy the Duck while at Epcot.

In April we went out to sea for four days. Then, later in the month, we went out again for two weeks. At one point we pulled alongside the French aircraft carrier Foch. It was an impressive sight, seen from our flight deck.

In May of 1990 the ship's dentists worked ashore at various dental clinics for two weeks while the Dental Department's decks were ripped up so a new deck could be installed. I worked at the Naval Dental Center during this time. When I returned to the ship after being away, it was mid-May and a major Change of Command ceremony was going to be held on the flight deck. I parked my car in the enormous lot and set my eyes upon the massive aircraft carrier in the distance. She was decorated with a red, white and blue banner lining the periphery of the flight deck, thick ropes securing her to the pier. Adjacent to her sat the mighty battleship, USS Iowa, the ship which had suffered an explosion in its number two 16-inch gun turret in April of 1989, killing forty-seven crewmen. The turret had erupted in flames during a routine training exercise about three-hundred miles northeast of San Juan, Puerto Rico.

Seeing the USS Kennedy again after having been away made me exclaim to myself, "What a magnificent ship!" Admiral Frank B. Kelso II was leaving CINCLANTFLT (Commander in Chief, U.S. Atlantic Command) to become the Chief of Naval Operations in Washington, D.C. Admiral Leon A. Edney was to replace him. During the ceremony, remarks were made by General Colin L. Powell, U.S. Army, Chairman, Joint Chiefs of Staff.

General Powell presented that day wearing black plastic-framed glasses—not the wire-framed ones the nation would know him to wear later when he was to become one of the stars of the Persian Gulf War, after which he was to be considered a top contender for President of the United States, although he decided, after much consideration, not to run for the office at the time.

In his comments, General Powell said the following: "Ladies and Gentlemen, just take a moment to look around this ship. Note the calm. Note the silence. Nowhere do we see that great beehive of flight deck activity of *Top Gun* fame that to the uninitiated, such as myself, looks like total chaos. The roar of jet engines is absent today. The sudden scream of the steam catapult doesn't split the air. The almost five acres of CV-67's flight deck lie at rest awaiting the wind and the sea and to be underway to demonstrate once again to a watching world that the United States is always ready to show to friends and to show to adversary alike that the Atlantic force is on guard. At rest, USS John F. Kennedy reminds us only vaguely that at sea she becomes a masterfully controlled fighting machine of awesome power. But we know the real secret of her power and we know that it is not located somewhere mysterious, somewhere deep in the spaces beneath us. No, the secret of her awesome power is all around us. It is in the people who designed her, the people who built her, and the people who sail her. And I must add it is in the American people everywhere, all across this great land and over sea because an aircraft carrier symbolizes a nation, the nation at sea and on guard, jealous of its freedom and its peace. We know too that such a combination of people is unbeatable. Such a combination is what gives to Admiral Frank Kelso's Atlantic Command its tremendous power, the power to deter war, and the power to promote peace. Such a power for peace has helped bring the world to the point we witness today where Secretary Baker is in Moscow so that in less than two weeks' time the leaders of the two superpowers can sit down and talk, talk about possibilities that less than twelve months ago we all would have thought unbelievable . . ."

On 31 May 1990, I checked out and was bonged off the ship. My tour of duty had ended. The following day, the USS Kennedy got underway for a deployment to New York City and Boston. I drove out to the Chesapeake Bay Bridge-Tunnel with a borrowed camcorder where I waited to film her as she passed by. When she appeared on the horizon, I smiled. During the two years I was attached to the ship, we were at sea about half the time. There were many memories. As she neared and I heard the frenetic 1MC announcements directing the beehive of activity that was out there, suddenly she appeared to me to be nothing more than a cold, gray hunk of metal populated by a bunch of kids playing Mickey Mouse games. In that moment I could not believe I had actually lived in such a dreary place for as long as I did. For an instant I felt relieved that I did not have to go out there again. The ship slowly passed by as it headed out to where she belonged, on the rugged oceans of the world.

But that feeling was fleeting. Perhaps I was too carelessly hasty in brushing her aside with such misplaced ease. Later in the day when I played back what I had filmed, I began to remember how beautiful she really was. And I appreciated how important she was to the nation. And then I knew I had left a piece of my heart out there on that ship.

Following her visit to New York City and Boston, she would return to her homeport and then abruptly depart to Desert Shield and Desert Storm, where she would be deployed for at least seven months, during which time the flight deck would become dangerously slick as the non-skid wore down from all the sorties launched to attack Iraq.

Now it is years later. I think back to the days I stood on the deck admiring the smooth glassy blue ocean, always knowing that at a moment's notice it could quickly change to a sea of turbulence to be feared and respected. I miss that.

I also miss the camaraderie of being stuck together as part of an expedition crew in some remote area of the world. And I long for the scent of JP-4 and the open ocean.

But that is all in the past now. At least today I can take comfort when I read the words spoken by John Kennedy on August 1, 1963: "Any man who may be asked in this century what he did to make his life worthwhile . . . can respond with a good deal of pride and satisfaction, *I served in the United States Navy.*"

REFERENCES

On the eve of the one-hundredth anniversary of the United States Navy Dental Corps, I would like to acknowledge all the people who have served in this organization.

There were many pamphlets, periodicals, personal notes, naval instructions, and other sources of information consulted in the building of this book. Particularly noteworthy references included:

Battle Station Sick Bay by Jan K. Herman (1997; Naval Institute Press)

Ship's Doctor by Capt. Terrence Riley (1995; Naval Institute Press)

Naval Operations in the 80's by Michael Skinner (Presidio Press)

Dental Care Aboard a United States Aircraft Carrier by Stephen Wylie Wallace (1991; Dental Corps International; Vol. 3, No. 1/91)

Supercarrier by George C. Wilson (1986; Macmillan Publishing Company)

The Dental Corps of the United States Navy—a Chronology 1912-1987 (The 75th Anniversary Committee, Inc.)

United States Ship John F. Kennedy Mediterranean Cruise 1988-89; Note that some of the ship's statistics were obtained from this source, but vary slightly from some of the measurements provided in the ship's brochures.

Dental Readiness of our Operating Forces by LCDR James A. Bowen and CDR James T. Judkins (March 1987; Clinical Update, Vol. 9, No. 3, Naval Dental School, Bethesda, Maryland)

And finally, thank you to Bertha and Devin Trently. And thanks to Chief, the neighbor's cat, who stayed up with me one late night to inspire me to push this project to its completion.